SHANNON

SHANNON

J.T. Bunn

This book was printed in the United States of America.

To order additional copies of this book, contact:
Xlibris Corporation
1-888-795-4274
www.Xlibris.com
Orders@Xlibris.com
33972

CONTENTS

Chapter 1   Beginning...7

Chapter 2   River Days..23

Chapter 3   Freighting Days 41

Chapter 4   Logan's Valley 60

Chapter 5   Frontier Justice 69

Chapter 6   Last Cattle Drive 77

Chapter 7   Lost Love..101

Chapter 8   Range War...124

Chapter 9   Final Battle 137

CHAPTER 1

Beginning

Shannon only talked of that day once, but he carried the memory of the events with him every day of his life. The traumatic events of that one day determined his future, one launched in savagery and youthful despair. It was a day of infamy, which would ever be for him the present past. On that day forces were set into motion, which would propel him into the mainstream of the westward movement.

On high tops, icy winds caressed fir and hemlock-crowned peaks with frigid lips, creating a halo of glistening rime frost. Below, mists hung over high valleys whose forests, already in autumn coats of many colors, acted out on nature's stage their final summer performance of the play *Indian Summer.* Freshening breezes crept softly through the coves, their chilling edge a portent of winter to come. Above Clingmans Dome a solitary bald eagle soared majestically in early morning updrafts. Its cry announced its presence to the small creatures below as they fed-on-mast in preparation for winter's scant fare.

Yet the quietude of every waking day was broken by the incessant pounding of the stamp mill on Hanging Dog Creek. Ore in small crudely built, somewhat efficient, blast furnaces turned out the raw materials of war. Ingots to be reforged into cannon barrel and shell, sword and knife, bayonet and rifle, at the foundries of Chattanooga were stacked in orderly rows. From the crucibles, molten metal poured in slow syrupy streams into waiting molds. In a close by cave there was the making of powder and rolling of fuse.

Though no major battles, only minor skirmishes, had occurred in the hills, war in a different form ravaged the Smokies. From the southern extremes of the Shenandoah to the red clay hills of Georgia, bushwhackers waged campaigns of vengeance and hate. The cataclysmic rift between North and South, Federal and Confederate had created an enmity, bitter and savage. It was a contest of unleashed emotions deadlier by far than any unrelenting blood feud.

From the ore pits or powder cave, where Shannon daily toiled, extracting ore and rolling fuse while others blended powder, the path to his tree-shrouded cabin rose steadily upward through stands of fir, hickory, oak, chestnut, and hemlock. It crossed two bold streams banked with laurel- and moss-covered rocks.

The first creek was his washbasin. Stripping, he would carefully place a small powder horn by his clothes. Icy waters from the peaks set his teeth chattering. Goose bumps rose and shivers caused him to do a jig. He dressed as quick as Jack-Be-Nimble and carefully tied his powder horn to his belt.

For Shannon the ritual was the same every day because it was downright shaming for a hulky thirteen-year-old boy to be dragged to the creek by the ear and rub-a-dub-dubbed until as pink as a baby's backside. Aenid, his mother, was a staunch believer in soap and forgiveness. She had absolutely no tolerance for dirt or sin.

Such thoughts of his mother were neither disrespectful nor slighting. She was simply wide on morals and long on cleanliness. It was something untelling how much he loved his ma and pa.

Shannon's pa was pure, unadulterated Irish. Fact was, he must have been kissed by the Blarney Stone rather than the other way around. He was a man filled with laughter most of the time but could have an unreasoning temper when riled. On the other hand, he was learned and gentle, with an incredible physical strength, which matched the inquisitive nature of his mind. Standing over six and a half feet he towered above others. All about said, when Shaun Murphy put his hands on most anything, it moved.

Shannon's mother was an equally arresting person. She stood six feet. Fair of face and statuesque of body, she turned every appreciative male eye in her direction. She was pleasing to look at with winsome smile and eyes of shimmering blue. Like spun gold her braided hair framed her head. Shannon felt she was about the prettiest thing one's eyes could feast upon.

His pa told and retold the story of how Aenid, his mother, came into his life. He had gone down to Charleston where the ships came into port from across the sea. There weren't but a few things Shaun Murphy liked better than a drink of good liquor; and that was a good, clean, knuckle-busting, head-knocking, jaw-rattling fight. As the story goes, he went into a tavern to buy the first and hopefully be presented the second free. He walked into the waterfront dive as sober as a Methodist preacher on the Sabbath, only to see a ship's captain backed to the bar by three waterfront thugs. The one holding a knife to the captain's stomach was talking.

"Fambro, I've waited two long years to catch you off the deck of your ship so as to get my pound of flesh. Put me in the brig on short rations, you did. Then at port put me ashore keeping part of my wages to pay for the two stinking casks of rum I took from your stores," the man holding the knife said.

Fambro, with utter contempt for his assailant, spoke in an even voice of command to his former second mate, "Come to your senses, man, and put that knife down."

"Keep your mouth shut, Fambro," the man replied. "I'll get my wages you took and more. I see a fat money pouch hanging from your belt. Empty that pouch on the bar or feel the bite of my steel."

Fambro's answer was an ultimatum. "You, bilge scum. Put down that knife, and I'll beat you to death just playing with you," Fambro said.

"That ain't the way of it. I've got the knife and me friends. You ain't holding a single card," The man replied.

The way his pa told the story, he felt the odds just weren't right; that is, for the three would-be bad men. His pa could be sort of sudden at times. Stepping behind the knife brandisher, he picked him up, shook him like a dog would shake a rag doll, and slammed him into the other two. Then his pa went to work in earnest. One he caught in a rolling hip lock but didn't turn loose the arm. That sometimes tears an arm out of the socket, and on this occasion it did. Within seconds he had sufficiently abused the other two.

Standing the next day before the magistrate, his pa pleaded his own case, using what might be called a religious defense. To each charge he pleaded, "The devil made me do it."

"So the devil made you do it, you say," questioned the magistrate, "made you tear a man's shoulder half off, crack the jaw of another, and permanently scar the scalp of another. Is that it?"

"Yes, Your Honor," his pa answered.

"Then tell me, did the devil make you shave the head of one of your opponents and carve your initials in his scalp with your bowie knife?" the magistrate asked.

"That was my idea, Your Honor," his pa answered in a patently honest manner.

His pa said the courtroom erupted with laughter; and his case was dismissed with a modest fine, which was paid by Captain Fambro.

John Fambro, the man whom his pa had defended, was a highly respected ship captain. As they sat talking, following the brief trial, Fambro told his pa about an indentured female servant on board his ship and his new second mate, who was as coarse and as vile as a scoundrel who ever lived. The mate came from a powerful and wealthy English family, who had urged Fambro to sign him on in hopes of making a man of him. Given to licentiousness, the man had tenaciously pursued the indentured woman to satisfy his lust.

One late night, Captain Fambro saw Halstead going below decks where the indentured and debtors were cabined. Following, with the first mate, he saw Halstead enter the barracks cabin, "cat footing" it to the bunk of Aenid. He clapped one hand over her mouth, pinned her to the bunk, and began to rip her clothes. Captain Fambro jerked him upright.

"Clap him in irons for the rest of the passage. If it weren't for your family, you would taste the cat-of-nine-tails," Fambro ordered. His stern Anglican theology caused him to continue in a voice sharpened by anger.

"You, sir, are a disgrace to your family and to this ship," Fambro continued. "You may be assured that I will inform the entire crew of your conduct. A complete report of your indiscretions will be forwarded to your family and the admiralty court. Remove yourself, sir, from my presence."

Fambro's sense of command and standards for officers serving under him permitted him to do nothing less, even though it broke with the general customs of time, which protected British peerage. He had long held in contempt those of privilege and power, who felt themselves above the laws of God and common decency.

Shortly afterward one of the crew told the captain that Halstead had been scheming to steal Aenid's papers. Fambro resolved that such would not be her fate, at Halstead's hands or any other like him.

Shannon's pa listened to Fambro's story. He sat quietly for a while and then he spoke to the captain, "I'll willingly buy her papers if she will come of her own free will to the hills and be my wife. I give you my word; she'll be treated with dignity and respect for that's the way of me and my kin."

"Then tell me," Fambro said, "other than the purchase price, what do you have to offer? Can you afford her a decent home?"

"I'll give her as good and as respected a name as there is in the hills," Shannon's pa replied. "There's a considerable cabin of hand-hewn poplar logs, snug and warm. There's a cow, two mules, and two beeves in the high pasture, a vegetable garden, bee gums and apple trees. It's as pretty a homestead as you'll find in the Smokies. Below there's a few acres cleared for crops; buckwheat, corn, barley and tobacco."

You mustn't think of Shannon's pa as one of those unknowing fellows who would buy a pig in a poke. It so happened his pa had walked the wharfs the day before. Coming upon a ship, he saw the most fetching woman he ever laid eyes on. As he stood staring at her she turned and looked at him. When their eyes met, his pa said his heart skipped a beat. Standing near her on the deck was the ship's captain, none other than Captain Fambro.

Early the next morning his pa went aboard ship. He entered the captain's cabin and met his ma for the first time. Within minutes his pa had paid for her papers from the small store of gold nuggets he had hoarded for years. They had been found here and there in his journeys across the Carolana Colony especially along Tick Creek. Vows were read, and Aenid became Shannon's would-be ma.

On deck Halstead furiously confronted them. About him was the look of a madman fueled by an uncontrolled temper. Shannon's pa held his peace until Halstead called his ma an unmentionable name. His pa then grabbed him by the front of his officer's tunic and commenced to slap him back to reasonable sanity. The captain and the deckhands finally pulled his pa off. By that time, however, his pa had somewhat rearranged his face.

That was the last they saw of Halstead. His parting shout, "I'll kill you if it takes me the rest of my life," rang in Shaun Murphy's ears as he and Aenid left the ship.

None knew better than the Irish the unreasoning vendettas of those high station, who had been humbled by commoners. That harsh lesson had been learned at the hands of the British. Irish immigration to America was not so much to escape the potato famine as it was to find freedom from British oppression: economic and political. They were little more than pawns to be controlled at the whim of the landed gentry and monetary power brokers. Before leaving for the hills, word came that Halstead, with the help of accomplices, had escaped from custody and absconded with the ship's strongbox.

Aenid brought to the marriage a unique strength comparable to that of Shaun. There was something wondrously different about her. Viking blood flowed in her veins. When the storm clouds gathered, dark and threatening, skipping lightning from peak to peak, making the thunder roll through cove and valley, Aenid would leave the cabin. With skirts gathered up, she would run to the craggy, rock cliff face above their cabin. As the wind and rain molded her dress to her body, she would lift her arms facing into the storm's swirling clouds and cry out, "Odin! Odin! Odin, the Norse god of battle." Odin, "the Invincible" was called upon by Shannon's mother to be his protector. This did not set too well with the few Scotch Presbyterians living nearby, who heard of its occurrence.

When it happened, Shannon felt an unbelievable surge of icy stillness. Then there came over him a fierce and terrible uncaring lust for battle. Aenid told him that the Viking blood ran hot within him. She cautioned him in hushed tones of the ever-lurking spirit of his ancestry that could cause him to erupt into a deadly icy rage.

Shannon inherited the best of two worlds, his pa's awesome physical strength, humor, love of life, freedom, and justice, as well as his ma's mysteriously unique spirit and lineage. At thirteen, he was a man who had grown and feared no thing or person. Yet he had a healthy respect for a capricious nature: book learning and especially the admonition of the good book.

Coming up to the cabin from the powder caves below, Shannon saw his ma on tiptoes, staring down the valley. This she did time and again, day after endless day, since his pa walked down that trail to fight the war.

Shannon's father was a strong believer in the Union, yet could not turn against friends and neighbors who were secessionists. To him the principle of equal justice for all men and corporate good so long as individual rights were protected, meant everything. Sitting by the fire at night, he would tell how the Union was like a rope woven of many strands. Each strand could hold, pull or carry only so much weight. But when all strands were woven together, the combined strength was greater than the sum of each strand working independently. He would argue that when any strand was taken away, the entire rope was weakened.

Shannon's feeling was that rope or no rope, he didn't want his pa to go off to war. But, go he did.

"Shannon, boy," his ma said, "see anything moving along the Winding Stairs?" Every night the same question. She was just hoping that he might see Shaun coming home. How they both wished him back. One quick glance below and Shannon's customary no spilled out. There did, however, seem to be a speck of something inching along the trail in the valley, which stretched out for a handful of miles below. Whatever or whoever it was could wait. Shannon had chores to do and a supper to eat. He didn't aim to be late for hunger was upon him.

Long strips of streak of lean and streak of fat were sizzling and popping in the hearth fry pan. Laid out on a clean sack was a pile of hoecakes ready for cooking on a hot rock in the ashes. They busied themselves, Aenid cooking and Shannon bringing. From the springhouse came a cake of butter and a crock of cold milk, the gifts of Old Bess, the cow. A jug of black strap molasses accompanied them on the table that had three plates and forks. At every meal, Shaun's place was set, ready and waiting. It was sort of a hoping thing.

Coffee, if it could be called that, made from roasted acorns and a liberal pinch of chicory, as well as the fry meat, sent a pleasing aroma through the cabin. In the midst of it all, Shannon's black dog Yona set to yowling like crazy. At first he thought Yona was calling for his share of the hoecakes. Then he realized the sound was different, wistful-like.

When Shannon stepped outside to see what in tarnation was going on, he was greeted by the most pitiful and wonderful sight a body could behold. Turning through the gate and headed for the porch was the almighty, spavined, ganted-up mule this side of perdition. Astride was a man who looked worse than the mule. He looked like he had been drawn through a knothole and left for crow bait. Spreading across his face, however, was a smile half a mountain high and twice a river across.

"How are you, boy?" he spoke as he slid from the saddle.

Shannon let out a yell one could have heard to the top of the gorge. "Ma, it's Pa!"

There was hugging and kissing and crying and drying. What a homecoming. Shannon's pa sat down at the table, said grace, and commenced to eat. Lordy, how that man ate. Shannon's ma finally stopped him, fearing he'd do himself harm. All of a sudden he collapsed, arms and head on the table. He was fast asleep from fearsome weariness.

Shannon's ma whispered, "Shannon, take care of the mule and bring your father's things in while I build up the fire and cover him with a blanket."

That poor mule was as tired as his pa and almost as hungry. Lifting off the worn-out saddle was not a problem. Two gunnysacks roped together and padded with rags were a different matter. Shannon was amazed at their weight. No wonder that mule was so tired. After putting the bags in the rear corner of the barn, Shannon walked out into the night. It was thinking time. Not to mention the fact that he was not so dumb as to think his pa would not sleep long when all he had dreamed about was coming home and holding his ma once again.

Shannon didn't rightly know how to speak no thanksgiving, so he simply told God he admired him for his pa's safe homecoming and if there was ever anything he could do for God, he'd do better. Shannon was so all-fired happy right then he would have promised God anything.

Night, inky dark or moon bright, was Shannon's friend. Many were the times he stepped boldly into the night, moving with the shadows, watching the coon and opossum on their nightly adventures. Or moving soundlessly, he'd creep to the edge of the tall grass in a high mountain meadow then moving into its depth to watch the deer browse.

Amble Walkingstick, his Cherokee friend, and he would play a game of hunter and hunted from dark thirty to light thirty. All through the reaches of the snowbirds they moved as silent warriors, neither catching a glimpse nor hearing a sound from the other. The deep woods were their training grounds where they learned the ways of the predator by day and night. The scream of the panther, snort of the deer, howl of the wolf, rumble of the buffalo, chatter of the squirrel, buzzing of the rattlesnake, and the weird trumpeting of elk were as familiar to them as the Cherokee language, spoken and sign, which they would use.

He and Amble from earliest memories had been constant companions but almost inseparable since Shannon's pa had gone off to war. Now that his father was home things would change, but how much, Shannon never realized at that moment.

In the cabin Shannon slipped up the loft ladder and drifted to sleep lulled by the comforting sound of his ma and pa speaking their love for each other. Shannon whispered to himself, *I don't know if the good book says anything about it or not, but it ought to speak to the good fortune of a boy whose parents love each other.*

The night should have rightly ended with the smell of cooking from the fireplace and the rousements of morning coming from the stable. Rather, it was an awakening to the pounding of hoofs, bullets smashing windows, eerie flickering light from bushwacker torches, and angry shouts from attackers.

"Traitor! You rotten traitor! Turned against your own. The boys in blue didn't get you but we will."

How they knew his pa had gotten home was a puzzlement to Shannon; but there were spies everywhere, and hatreds ran deep and strong.

With the first hail of bullets to hit the cabin Shannon scrambled from the loft. As he did a glass shard hit him, leaving a bloody streak, only skin deep, from ear to chin. His foot got caught in a rung of the ladder, sending him plunging to the floor. There he lay dazed and unmoving.

Seeing Shannon fall, Aenid screamed and stood to cross the floor to him. At that moment a second volley of rifle fire slashed through windows and door. Without a sound Aenid fell to the floor beside Shannon. Death had come swift and certain.

Shannon, now fully alert after his fall, could not speak. His pa crawled across the floor and gathered the limp form of Aenid in his arms. Shannon looked at him seeing unbelievable anguish and misery.

In a broken, grief-stricken voice, Shaun spoke, "Boy, you listen good. Ain't time to tell you but once. First off, don't forget the rock. Remember now, don't forget the rock. Now you go out the tunnel trapdoor to the stable. Get the bags I brought home with me. Put them in the tunnel. Block both ends like I showed you. Don't come out for nothing until it's safe. Unchink the spy holes. Make sure those murderous devils are gone before you move. Look in the bags. In them are things you'll need."

Shannon at first thought it was his ma's blood on his pa's shirt. There was a spreading stain, and Shannon knew his pa had been hit and hit hard.

"Pa, you're bad hurt, and Ma ain't moving. I'm not about to leave you," Shannon cried out.

"Son, you are all the gather me and your ma will ever have. Don't disappoint me," his pa said, gasping. "You've got to live. If you die, we are cut off from the land of the living. Now, you get going and don't look back. Make your ma and pa proud of you, because we will be looking on according to the good book. Stand straight and tall. Look man and God in the eye unashamed. Never forget who you are." Shaun then slumped over, eyes open in death.

Snatching a left-over corn pone from the table along with a few pieces of side meat, Shannon dropped through the trapdoor and into the tunnel. It was darker than midnight in an ivy thicket in the tunnel.

Years before some unknown had dug a small quartz-laden gold vein until it petered out. In the short shaft Shaun had found a few flecks of gold. It must have been one of those freaks of nature. Wisely, Shaun had built the cabin backed up to the tunnel mouth. Then he drilled through to the surface where he laid out a barn of hand-hewn poplar logs. A small trickle of water ran from the tunnel into the barn trough. By building in such a manner Shaun had created an escape route, from cabin to barn, completely unseen and unknown by others.

To slip into the barn and back into the tunnel with his pa's makeshift saddlebags only took a few minutes. But his heart was not in it. It was in the cabin with his ma and pa.

Suddenly it boiled up within him, that terrible rage his ma told him would come. What happened next shook Shannon like rolling thunder shaking the hills. The rage turned into icy dead calm, frightening in its power and unyielding in its grip. Possessing him was the urge to destroy, to make those who had murdered his ma and pa pay, and pay dearly.

With both ends of the tunnel blocked, Shannon carefully eased the stone peg from one of the peepholes. Immediately there came the smell of smoke. They were burning the cabin.

Shannon had heard many a time that men don't cry. If that was the case he wasn't a man. Slumping against the cold stone passageway with head cradled in arms, tears flowed and sobs racked his body.

Again that awesome thing happened. Shannon wondered if he was awake or dreaming, *Was it real or imagined?* A picture materialized before him. It was nebulous and distorted yet clear of meaning. A gigantic warrior, with taunting curses and contemptuous laughter, was wreaking horrible carnage. He was sweeping the battlefield front and left with a monstrous clamor. Beside him was a blond blue-eyed amazon girded in the leathers of a huntress. On her head was a horned helmet and in her hand a bloody battleaxe that fell the enemy front and right. From her lips came the cry of Odin and from his the deadly incantations of the Druids. As the apparition faded Shannon heard the words, "You are our son. In your veins flow our blood."

From the peephole the bushwhackers were clearly to be seen. It was Tob Messer and his villainous crew. The fire's glow lighted the night and their faces were crystal clear. They were passing around a jug of white, congratulating themselves on a job well done.

"Killed the whole lot. Got Aenid and Shaun as well as their get. The colonel will pay and pay well for this job.

The colonel's name was not mentioned, but Shannon promised himself and the good Lord that someday he would know. That would be a day of reckoning, for he planned a "come to Jesus" meeting with him.

Pulling over his pa's "trampaddik" and stretching out, Shannon did what Shaun had written he did during lulls in battle. He wrote how nobody, not even "Jeb" Stuart, could understand how he slept at a time like that. His pa indicated he would ride right into hell with Jeb Stuart if he had a ten-minute nap. In fact, he wrote that if a person had ever ridden into the mouth of Yankee cannon, they had ridden into the maws of hell.

When Shannon awoke, he checked the peepholes. It was graying dawn and time to crawl from his grave. He wasn't dead and soon enough Tob Messer and his crowd would find it out.

A quarter mile from the cabin was a cache. His pa had discovered the small cave hidden in an ivy thicket. It was high and dry. There they kept emergency supplies in event of an Indian raid from north Georgia or the far northeastern tribes. Two possible bags hung by their straps. Each was filled with powder, shot, steel, flint, and tinder. There was also a tinker-made knife, pemmican, pouch of cornmeal, mush makings containing a pinch or two of cinnamon and a lump of sugar. The mush pouch had to be replaced from time to time to keep it fresh. Strips of rawhide, a small packet of cut-to-length turkey feather fletches for arrows, fish hooks, a coil or two of line, little packets of doctoring herbs, small tin of rendered ground hog grease mixed with soothing herbs, and three or four handmade waxed bow strings completed the whole kit and caboodle. The bags had been made using triple layers of heaviest leather. This would provide leather for making extra moccasins when needed. There was something else, however, that only Shannon knew about.

Shannon emptied his pa's saddle packs. There were gifts for Aenid and him. Tears tried to come again, but Shannon had cried out.

Can a body cry until it can't cry any more? Shannon thought. He guessed it could. His ma's packages he put aside, never to be opened. In his was a pair of brown sailcloth pants along with a belt and holster that held a strange-looking pistol marked LeMat.[1] In the other packs was a Henry .44 rifle and shells, a Spencer rifle, a Remington revolver, an Arkansas toothpick, sharp as a razor, and a small deerskin pouch with six twenty-dollar gold pieces. His pa had done some almighty scrounging along the way.

Shannon laid out what he would need for light and fast traveling as well as what he intended to give to his friend Amble. The only plan he had was to travel far and find the place his pa had talked about with such longing on many a cold winter's night.

One night in particular, Shannon recalled the telling of the accounts of Jedediah Strong Smith's journey of 1826-1827. He was a mountain man, noted for carrying a Bible and a butcher knife, who endlessly talked of a far high mountain valley watered by twin streams, graced with game and lush grass to which someday he would return.

As far as Shannon was concerned his pa turned into another man as he spun the yarns of mountain men who were his kin—men who had walked the high, lonesome searching, reaching and stretching to touch the far horizon. The times and the exploits of men such as John Coulter, and Manuel Lisa, Jim Bridger and James Clayman, Jedediah Smith and Joseph Walker; when talked about, produced a wandering gleam in his pa's eyes. With such men Shaun Murphy would have been at home, especially his own grandfather, Irish Murphy who, back in the 1840s had spent a year among the Cheyenne. It was Irish who had found a white buffalo calf and carried it to the Cheyenne.

---

[1]   Nine hundred LeMat handguns were delivered to Confederate forces. It is reported that J. E. B. Stuart as well as other high-ranking Confederate officers favored the Le Mat as a personal weapon.

It was a totem of great good fortune, and Shannon's grandpa was revered by the tribe from that time until he left the land of the Cheyenne.

Shannon's pa would never realize his dream. Maybe Shannon could do it for him because what he had in mind would surely make him high tail it out of the Smokies. There would be no time to tarry. He didn't intend to be like the roving preacher who visited with the women when the menfolk were gone and tarried too long.

From a niche, high on the cave wall, Shannon took down a small keg. Iron bound it was, with bunghole and peg stopper. Each day when he left the powder cave, he'd carry home with him a bit of powder. Slowly the keg filled, twenty-five pounds of dangerously volatile black powder.

Lon Mayhew, once a shipwright and gunner's mate had shown Shannon how to roll fuse. Many were the yarns he told of high-masted ships, the creaking timbers, wind playing in the halyards, pounding of cannon, moans of the wounded, acrid smell of burnt powder, and the stench of battle emptied upon the decks of oak.

Uncle Lon, as all the young men called him, was an expert on powder, shot, and fuse. Whenever he left a short length of fuse on a rolling slab, Shannon would scoff it up. When lighted, it sputtered and burned sending off tiny cascades of bright sparks. This was the only fireworks he had except for shooting the anvil. Now the fuse would serve another purpose—a deadly one.

What Shannon saw through the peepholes was etched in his memory. Every one of the attackers had, from time to time, sat by the fire and yarned away the night with his pa. All except Dave Renfroe had on one or more occasion pulled up to the Murphy's table and consumed a quail pie or hot johnnycakes covered with molasses. Renfroe had always been a loner, coming and going from the fringe of the Black Rock area. Some said he was an outlaw, who left the isolation of the high tops to prey upon unwary travelers and unprotected homesteads in the foothills. He was as mean as a cougar with a sore tooth. All shunned him except his pa. Yet there he was with others to whom his pa had extended the hospitality of their home.

Unbelievable is the power of greed. Shannon clearly heard Renfroe ask Tob how much pay they would get for the night's work. Tob Messer, the leader of the bushwhackers, Dave Renfroe, Tim Kelly, Handy McLauhlin, and Sandy Reese he saw clearly. Not only that but he had caught bits and pieces of their conversations. Word of his pa coming back to the mountains had somehow preceded him. More than one had said the war was lost before the fighting ended, and they headed home like his pa. Some would call it deserting; others would call it plain common sense. Tob Messer and his band of cutthroats had collected bounty on "home bounders" from the Union command in Knoxville area for months during the waning year of the war.

These home bounders were men who would leave the army, come home, and put in a crop so their families could survive the year then return to reenlist. Tob almost inevitably collected his bounty on dead men. But in this instance he had been hired to kill Shannon's entire family. Why?

The very thought of it hit a central nerve at the heart of the mountain way of life. Law and the courts came late to the Smoky Mountains. County seats like Waynesville, Sylva, and Murphy had their judges, courts, and high sheriffs. Back in the hollows, deep valley, and remote coves, however, justice was homespun. The legal code was the Old Testament put out by Justice King Jim. A jury composed of those of fierce independence, unyielding standards of right and wrong, as well as individual rights, heard every case. Verdicts were based on the law of retaliation, *lex talionis* (an eye for an eye and tooth for a tooth). From time to time fairness suffered at the hands of such a system because blood ran hot and hatred deep. Simply put, if one protected not their own, their own was not protected. Vindication for an offense, generally small or great, was the rule of the day. It was in these terms that Shannon thought and responded to the attackers.

Shannon heard the group agreed to meet at Sandy's cabin the next night, and he agreed it would be a night they would long remember.

What he planned might have been awfully troublesome to some folks' conscience but not to his. They had come upon his family at night with murder in their hearts. Retribution might belong to the Lord, but Shannon decided the Lord needed a bit of help along the way.

Shannon's pa used to jokingly say at times it was better to make a good run than a bad stand. What Shannon planned was a good stand and a good run. He wanted Tob Messer and his gang to get a king-size dose of nighttime medicine. If the dose was too strong and the patients died, then the world would be just that much better off.

The best Shannon could tell it, was about midnight when he left the cache. Under his arm was the long-hoarded keg of powder with fuse in place. In his mind was the anticipation of sweet revenge.

Sandy's cabin nestled on a hillside about two miles from Shannon's cave retreat. Moving in darkness, on moccasin feet, was old hat to Shannon. This was a different game, however, unlike the one Amble and he played in the Snowbirds. That was fun, this was war.

Stepping from the stand of hemlocks, Shannon eased toward the cabin. A celebration was afoot. Tim had unlimbered his fiddle, and the jug was being passed around. Buck, Sandy's bear dog, appeared out of nowhere, growling low in his throat, hair bristling across his shoulders. If there was one thing that Buck loved, it was corn pone and anybody who gave it to him. A chunk of corn pone big enough to choke a sow hog waved in front of him, set his tail wagging. Buck almost dehanded Shannon, snatching it from his fingers. He sank to the ground and began working it over.

Hand-adzed timbers suspended on slab rock pillars leveled the cabin on the downhill side, giving plenty of room to crawl underneath. Near the middle of the floor Shannon lashed the keg on the pillar's ledge next to the center floor joist. With match cupped in hand he lit the fuse.

All perdition broke loose. The fuse flared burning so fast it was a fright. Scrambling to get from under the cabin Shannon roused up Sandy's guinea hens. The raucous alarm set the whole world into motion. Buck got in between Shannon and the thicket and let out a howl when Shannon stomped all over him. At the same time those who had been drinking inside came helter-skelter, stumbling and falling, across the porch trying to get out to see what was happening. And in the midst of it all, with a mighty roar, the cabin just rose up in the air. Timbers went flying, the cook stove cartwheeled through the air, landing in the yard. A gigantic snow cloud of feathers from the exploding feather bed filled the air. Tob did comic acrobatics, soaring through the air with arms and legs askew. Sandy staggered about in the yard with only the fingerboard of the fiddle in one hand and a broken bow in the other. Renfroe, who had been sitting closest to the fireplace, crawled about in the yard, muttering oaths and slapping at the smoldering sleeves of his coat.

Sandy had come to rest wrapped around the base of a small chestnut tree. In between his moans and groans he confessed all to his maker because anything so cataclysmic as this had to be judgment day.

Tim Kelly was a crumpled heap. There was no movement. He made no sounds. Tim had started across the room and was directly over the charge when it blew.

Shannon had killed his first man, but never again would he take a life in any way but a fair stand-up fight.

Shannon didn't know that a keg of powder would do so much damage! He got out of there like a fox with his tail afire, leaving behind a mighty chorus of moaning and groaning and cussing.

Heading for the cache Shannon went by the still-smoking ruins of his homeplace, hoping to see if there was enough left of the bodies of his ma and pa for a decent burial. Close by were two fresh graves. On the freshly turned earth were faint imprints of moccasins. A lump rose in Shannon's throat almost choking him to death. Could Amble have done this? Then and there a vow was made. Such an act of kindness would never be forgotten by him or his. Someday, if it were Amble or any of the Cherokee who laid his folks to rest, they would be paid full measure and heaping over.

As Shannon turned his feet toward the trail, it seemed his pa spoke, "Boy, remember the rock. You're forgetting! Please, boy, remember the rock."

He turned so fast he almost fell. There wasn't but one rock that his pa had ever pointed out to him. It was the night his pa left to fight the war. The family was sitting by the fire, watching the flames dance their last dance before bidding good night.

"Boy, you see that funny-shaped rock on the chimney face?" his pa said. "Never forget it. If I don't come back from the war, you and your ma will need what's behind that rock. Promise me you won't ever forget it."

Easing around the still-smoking charred timbers, Shannon worked the rock out. In the hollow was a tin box wrapped in greased sailcloth tightly glued to the box. Looking up at that chimney Shannon somehow hoped it might stand forever, a silent sentinel over the graves of his folks. He slipped the rock back in place and turned his back on the only home he had ever known.

A short time later Shannon was at the cache. He quickly took up the possibles bag and moved off into the woods. Over one shoulder he slung the Henry rifle and on the other the possibles bag. The Arkansas toothpick was snugged in his high-laced moccasins. All the worldly goods he had were on his back and in his pockets. Yet in Shannon's mind and heart was the incomparable inheritance of two wonderful people.

One last visit with Amble, and he'd head over the Winding Stairs to Shooting Creek; from there was a trail to Hanging Dog. Shannon could then cut across the mountains to Sevierville in Tennessee. A shorter well-used route out of Georgia crossed the Cherokee Boundary (called Qualla Boundary) and the Smokies. It also wound up at Sevierville.

It was the way less traveled; however, that lured Shannon. Days of solitude, hours of steady climbing would weary the body and bring immediate and blessed sleep. Nights were the worst for they brought reoccurring nightmares of his ma and pa's deaths.

For Amble, Shannon had left a message. A coded sign in stones to meet him at the boundary tree. Moving without sound on a carpet of hemlock needles, Shannon came to the base of the giant tree and slipped under the branches. There were the things he had secreted when he left the markers. Hours went by; Shannon waited, knowing Amble would come when possible. His sign indicated danger, Amble would understand.

Shannon awakened with a start. The first light of day was just beginning. The call of a horned owl, promptly answered by a turkey gobbler on his roost, had roused him. Amble! Few are the folk who can talk so easily the language of the owl. Shannon's answer scarcely died when Amble walked up to the tree.

Their talk was brief. Wasting no time Shannon related the events of the past two days. This was done in Cherokee, a graphic language with precise word meanings. Then, for a long period of time they sat without speaking until Amble broke the silence.

"Hold long in memory your Cherokee brothers. Acknowledge the great spirits and seek their vision. Be a warrior who asks no quarter and gives no quarter. Find strength of your ancestors in you. Die a warrior's death as you live a warrior's life. We Cherokee are peaceful people but when aroused, become fearsome in battle. Be and do as we. Take Silent Killer, my bow. Take my arrows. Take my medicine bag. Take my blessings and those of my father and grandfather. Go now before the enemy comes."

Has ever a man or boy had such a friend? Reaching into his possibles bag, Shannon took out a tinker-made knife and from the crotch of the tree the Spencer rifle he had hidden the day before. These he handed to Amble. Only the eyes of Amble's stoic face expressed his inner excitement and appreciation. Each gave to the other the silent hand signal of farewell. Amble disappeared into the early morning mist. Moments later Shannon heard the eerie lonesome wail of the panther. He pushed back a rising floodtide of emotion and started his journey to find a future and build a life.

Ahead was the undiscovered to be found, the unknown to be known. Yet in a real sense the future was in the present. He never rightly understood what his pa meant when he said, "The future is now." Shannon was beginning to understand, however, that events occurring in his life at the moment were crowding the future in on him. Something like every new step being half in the present and half in the future. At times when he thought on such things, his mind just upped and bogged down. Deep inside he knew that for every ending there was a beginning. Shannon was not so unschooled that he did not know a setting sun was a rising sun somewhere else. As one day ended another began. A day in his life had ended but it was the beginning of another. He was trustful that a sad ending would bring a happy beginning. Thus, the odyssey began.

CHAPTER 2

River Days

Tennessee and Kentucky were behind. Before Shannon was the Ohio River, gateway to the South and barrier to the West. Passage from Carolina to Ohio had not been uneventful. It had been punctuated with hard lessons preparing him for proving days ahead.

Weeks of solitude, of lonely travel through primal forests, began to form the man Shannon was to be. His boyish frame began to fill out for any Smoky Mountain boy with shot and powder lived well in the lush forests. His favorite time was evening camp. He drank in the sounds of the night critters as the fire coals glowed red while pondering the past, present, and future. Thinking was a mighty powerful pastime. There was plenty of time to churn the crock of hopes, dreams, and wishes, making the sweet butter of the future more palatable. Of course along the way he had come upon other movers but shied away, finding no one whose companionship he liked better than his own.

Hunting the white tail had taught him many a wise lesson. Wiley bucks never walked the main trail with the does, except during the rut when all caution was cast aside. Find the trail of the doe, then work the thickets on either side. There would be found the faint trail of the buck. Does in sight, bucks hidden. At open spaces does crossed first. When the buck saw it safe, he crossed. It didn't seem right but that was the way of nature. Shannon's way of going was that of the buck's, never on the main trial, path, or road, but in the woods parallel to them. The first time he broke the pattern he encountered a life-threatening situation.

Midway on the pike between Frankfort and Louisville was a stage stop, Christienberg, whose name belied its true nature. For miles the roadbed had deepened with banks six to eight feet rising on either side. Ancient oaks, ash,

23

and walnut trees spread their limbs, creating a canopy of green overhead. Several cabins dotted the top of a slight rise. Two buildings dominated the fledgling community: a tavern and a church. A short distance away was the Flood Plantation. The tavern's customers were a melting pot of the best and the worst humanity had to offer.

For half a day Shannon laid up observing all the coming and going. Nigh on to evening, cooking smells coming from the tavern near done him in. He hid his pack, taking only a boot knife and one twenty-dollar gold piece with him. That showed how almighty dumb a person could be. Shannon let his stomach rule his common sense. He headed for the tavern and stepped inside.

A bar ran halfway down one side of the room. Beyond was a huge fireplace with bubbling kettles of soup and stew suspended on hangers and meat roasting on spits. Shannon's stomach did a couple of whirligigs and then fair screamed "food!" For endless days he had eaten wilderness fare such as squirrel, rabbit, trout, and mush. A haunch of beef, crusty brown and dripping with sputtering fat, was as alluring to him as the Promised Land must have been to the Hebrew slaves from Egypt.

Moving past the bar he headed for the common tables at the far end of the room where eating had already commenced. Before realizing what was happening, he was tripped, sprawled full out on the floor. Looming above him was a man with the worst imaginable case of uglies.

"Lookie here. If it ain't another one of them movers a heading for the frontier," the man said. "Sonny, boy, you want to play mountain man with full-grown men?"

Shannon stretched out his hand to pick up the dropped gold piece. The man's boot was faster than his hand.

"Boy, get your grubby fingers off of my gold piece," the man ordered. "Didn't your folks tell you that it won't right to steal from honest folk?"

Standing up and brushing himself, it occurred to Shannon that it would be the proper thing to at least reply. Before he could speak a word his antagonist growled, "Git, boy! Don't bother to show your ugly face here again. If you do, I might have to lean on you." The men at the bar snickered, and Shannon's ire rose rapidly.

Shannon turned, saying, "Mister, I guess my innocent baby face has somehow offended you. My pa always told me to be respectable to my elders, and that is exactly what I intend to do."

Shannon's hands were huge, wrists thick. Working the drill and single jack along with the pick in the ore pits over a period of two years had callused his hands and broadened his shoulders. The loose fitting tunic hid the more than youthful rippling muscles of his chest and arms. Shannon's sweeping left backhand rocked his tormentor hard against the bar as his right hand whipped the Arkansas toothpick to the man's throat. The needle sharp point drew blood. A tiny streak of red ran across the rows of dirt in the grimy folds of his neck.

"Friend, have you ever seen how we stick hogs back in the hills? It shorely does make a mess. Well, sir, if you so much as twitch, I'm going to spill your blood all over this fine bar," Shannon cautioned him.

There was a scraping sound and the corner of Shannon's eye caught a flash of metal sliding on the bar. The man grabbed for the gun. It was pure simple reflex. Shannon's blade flashed from the man's throat, pinning his hand to the bar.

As memory faded, Shannon heard a choked off scream. Then there was a deafening blast, a split second of pain, and finally nothingness.

He came to shivering from cold, lying half in a swift-running icy stream, known in those parts as Elkhorn Creek. Shannon's head throbbed and roared as if it had a stamp mill running inside. One arm was badly bruised. Easing his hand to his head he discovered a crusty, matted furrow across his scalp. Stark reality hit him. He had been shot. The more awake he became the greater the pain. Wave after wave of intolerable spasms occurred. Every part of his body seemed to find it's own way to cause suffering. He brought one handful of water after another to his mouth. Loss of blood had created an incredible thirst. Slaking his thirst was not enough. Shelter and warmth meant survival, both had to be found. Crawling only inches to begin with, it took what seemed to be three lifetimes and part of an eternity to reach the overhanging trees along the creek bank. Consciousness came and went. It was full sun when he finally gained his senses. By noon he was feeling a little better.

Shannon wondered, *Was my lonely journey to end here in the muck like a wounded wild animal awaiting death?* Within him the furies began to rise. He resolved that no offspring of Shaun Murphy and Aenid Erickson would ever be put down like this.

Still belted tight at his waist was the possibles bag. In it was flint and steel. A Russell Green River clasp knife rested, snugged in a wet trouser pocket. Many had made do with less.

Fighting down the sickening pain he stripped the inner bark from a tree rubbing it almost into powder. More bark was peeled then rolled between his fingers to separate the fibers. Dry twigs were snapped from a nearby branch. Flint was laid to steel and sparks showered on the nest of tinder. A thin wisp of smoke arose as Shannon softly blew on the starter. A tiny tendril of flame peaked. It's hard to believe how much heat can come from a fire no bigger than a cake of corn bread.

Shannon cut a sheet of bark, rolled it into a cone, and laced it between a forked stick with a strip cut from his deerskin tunic. It made a handy cup in which to heat water. So long as it was held well above the fire, and the flame did not rise above the level of the water the bark would not burn. It was one of those clever inventions of man for time past memory.

The first heating Shannon drank; then the second and third. After that, cup after cup was heated and poured on his tunic and britches to ease the pain and make it possible to peel leather tunic and leggings from clotted wounds.

Moving the few feet from the willows to the creek bank for water became easier each trip. Building up the fire Shannon pulled off his clothes and moccasins. Propped up on sticks to dry, they let off small clouds of steam while he turned them from front to back, soaking in the fire's warmth. Fearing the leathers would shrink if dried too long he somehow wrestled them on. The moist heat was almighty comforting to his bruised body. He learned from a Cherokee healer that a willow tree's inner bark boiled in water and the solution drunk would relieve pain. A cup of bitter brew did seem to help.

On the last trip for water Shannon's eyes scanned every inch of the opposite riverbank. At one point a sheer rock cliff, some twenty-five to thirty feet, rose above the water. Flashing through his mind came a hazy image of falling, hurtling head-over-heels in the air, dropping toward water below. It was plain. The sound he heard before passing out was a shot. He had been shot and thrown over the cliff into the water.

Uncontrollable anger surged through Shannon. Find his weapons! Go back to the tavern! Kill every mother's son that comes out the door! They were all guilty for none had come to his defense. As the furies raged within him memories from the past made themselves known.

Two hollows over from the cabin where he was born there lived an old woman, Granny Sills. Although snaggled of tooth, hollow of face, and bent of body, her mind was like a steel trap and her tongue sharper than a well-honed razor. Many times his pa had sent him over to her cabin with a haunch of venison or turkey freshly killed. Granny Sills would say, "Thank ye and then set ye." Out would come a cake of corn pone and a jug of molasses. As eating commenced she instructed Shannon in wise ways. Aenid had read to him about Egyptians who had schools of wisdom where they taught the young princes of Egypt. Shannon was dead sure those wisdom teachers had the strangest names he had ever heard like Imhotep and Hordedef. Granny's wisdom, on the other hand, was the homegrown type.

"Man child," she'd say, "there is honor in feuding only if'n you kill the guilty ones. Killing them—what's without guilt—will haunt you night and day. What's more, you'll conjure up every smidgen of what happened and the guilties will grip you something awful."

"But, Granny, how do you know who is and who isn't guilty?" Shannon asked.

"Boy, in the woods you don't shoot at sounds, twitching bushes, or blurred glimpses of something moving in the dawning or darkening. You make sure what you're shooting. Before you kill man or beast you make sure who or what it is, and know for pure certain that it oughta be kilt," she replied.

Shannon didn't actually know who shot him, he could only remember one face. It was the face of the man whose hand he had pinned to the bar, a face never to be forgotten. One eye drooped slightly. A livid scar ran across the eyebrow to his forehead. Of course on the back of his right hand would be the mark of Shannon's knife.

The words of Granny Sills made sense to him. *Perhaps the guilty ones had already left the tavern,* he thought. There were adventures to be experienced, faraway places to be explored, and dreams to be fleshed out and made real. Retaliation could wait. There was a majestic lure of a faraway valley, a homestead, maybe even a ranch.

After two days of searching, Shannon found his packs; and it bothered him greatly to leave without getting revenge. A body, however, could never tell what the future might hold. It would be ironic justice if, in the days ahead, he should chance upon one or all of those who attempted to kill him.

The future was nipping at his heels like a dog driving cattle. He set his face toward Louisville Town and walked across the threshold of a new day.

Back in the hills folks had heard talk of river flatboats, or barges, and keelboats. Both plied the trade of the Ohio and the Mississippi. His pa had told of barges which floated on the current, carrying tons of cargo, making one way trips to the end of the river at a place called New Orleans. There they were dismantled and sold as lumber.

The keelboats, however, not only went down river but back up the river.

Regardless of what Shannon had been told he wasn't ready for what he saw and heard as he came upon the river. Along with everything else there were huge boats with paddle wheels in the back. When one cut loose with its steam whistle, it scared the "bejiggers" out of him.

Before he went down into that mass of confusion, Shannon had some thinking to do. Walking upstream he finally found a quiet, shady grove of giant beech trees with a nearby spring. Maybe the fates would help him decide what to do.

Shannon recalled Old Man Ayscue, who lived on the bottomland and spent most of his time yarning at McKinney's store, better known by most local folks as Loafer's Glory. It was told among the hill folks that he was highly educated, having gone to one of those big colleges back East to study for ministry; but his dedication to theology, however, was overcome by his devotion to strong drink.

One day, with his faithful listeners gathered about, he told of a Roman general who consulted sacred chickens when he was about to engage the enemy. His troops were on a ship, so he put food out on the deck for the sacred chickens. If they ate, it indicated he would win a victory. If they refused to eat he would lose the battle. When he turned the chickens out they refused to eat. The general promptly threw them overboard with the admonition, "If you won't eat, then maybe you will drink." He then went on to win the battle even though the chickens predicted otherwise. So much for divination! Mountain people are long on superstition but short on ignorance.

On the other hand, his ma's story about such goings-on was surely a puzzler. Aenid said in the good book there was a writing by a fellow called Ezekiel. He wrote a story about a king of Babylon who came to a fork in the road and didn't know which way to take his army. His ma told him that the king tried to get an answer from his god by "shaking his quiver and consulting his liver." How he accomplished that no one seemed to know. His ma said it had something to do with the casting of lots. Shannon didn't have any chickens and had no idea where his liver was, so neither story was of any help.

As these and a thousand other things crisscrossed his mind, Shannon began unpacking his possibles bag. In the bottom was the tin box taken from the chimney. For a fairly slim box about as long as his foot it was quite heavy. The top was slightly rusted. When he pried it open, a shower of thick gold coins hit the ground in front of him. Shannon then knew why the box had been so heavy for its size. The coins looked old to him, real old. He had never seen any like them before. Gold had brought him trouble and near death before, and now it was staring him in the face again. Somehow he had to get it and himself to some safe place. From what he had observed of the Louisville waterfront from afar there seemed to be half the ruffians and would-be bad men of the Ohio present and accounted for.

In short order Shannon had a small fire going. The shaved jerky in a cup with a little hot water made a right passable broth. After eating he stretched out looking at the first stars of the evening through the limbs above and listened to the far-off river sounds. Shannon mused, *A body doesn't know how hard it is for a boy just past fourteen to make big, grown-up decisions.* His mind drifted back to his Smoky Mountain growing-up days. For a while Shannon just rested there, sifting the past through the sieve of memory.

For some reason Mr. Samuels came to his mind, and he smiled to himself. About once a year Samuels showed up, carrying a ponderous backpack. When he came, it was the most wonderful of times. Always he was a guest in the Murphy cabin. All about knew that Mr. Samuels was one the shrewdest but honest traders who walked in the hills. In fact, far and wide it was noised about that he could trade property with the devil and come out with the deed to hell, all legal and proper.

He was the best contact the mountain folk had with the outer world, since they were so isolated in the far coves. Not only did he bring the news but all sorts of trade goods. There were pretties the women longed for, like bows and scarves. There were also necessities such as needles, thread, buttons, awls, knives, hatchets, and some piece goods. His pack to them was a bottomless treasure trove.

After supper the neighbors would come for word passed quickly through the hills and hollows. Blankets were spread on the puncheon floor, and wall-to-wall people would spend the night. When the buying stopped the conversation began with the news of the outside world being the main topic of conversation.

On one such night, Mr. Samuels told how some of his family had almost moved out to Louisville at the insistence of Mr. Jacob Adler, a prominent businessman. As Shannon drifted off to sleep he resolved to find Mr. Adler, if at all possible, and ask his advice about what to do with the gold money.

A man-size hunger was upon him when he woke. If food could be found, there would be one horrendous feeding frenzy. It is untelling what Shannon could have done right then with a mess of fatback, a hatful of hoecakes, a jug of molasses or mountain honey, and about a number three washtub full of black coffee with a pinch of chicory. Yet he dared not show any of the coins, so feeding time would have to wait.

Chewing a piece of jerky, with belongings over his shoulder, Shannon walked toward the bustling waterfront. In the heart of the business district overlooking the waterfront was Adler and Sons. The building was substantial.

Its red brick walls rose some thirty feet above the street. Large windows of glass panes sparkled in the sunlight, not dingy and covered with cobwebs as others along the cobblestone street. Heavy oak shutters flanked each window. A series of four granite steps, worn on the edges, led up to twin massive doors of carved oak strapped with iron. On the lentil above the door were two words chiseled in the stone. The characters were curious, unlike anything Shannon had ever seen. Later he was told that it meant House of Adler. Without hesitation, Shannon climbed the steps and entered the door. With the first person encountered he made his inquiry.

"I'd like to have words with Mr. Jacob Adler, if at all possible," Shannon said. The reply was brusque.

"Just what is your business with Mr. Adler? He is an important man and cannot be bothered by just any person who walks in off the street," the man said.

"Mister, my business is personal and private, and if I hadn't heard of Mr. Adler from our family friend, Mr. Isaac Samuels, I wouldn't be here," Shannon replied.

He was startled by Shannon's firm reply; and a curious, but quite serious, expression swept across his face. In a most courteous and civil manner he said, "This way, young sir, I meant no offense."

He ushered Shannon into the office of Mr. Adler at the far end of a long room, which had desks and chairs along both sides of an aisle. At every workstation there were men scribbling something in huge books.

The man behind the big desk at the other side of a gold-lettered door was right out of the good book. Shannon had spent many a happy hour in Aenid's lap, looking at her Bible which had pictures of folks call patriarchs. Adler's bearded face was pleasant but strong. Although slight of stature he was broad of shoulder. A strong resonant voice was crisp with authority. His most arresting feature was his eyes. They penetrated, searched, and bored into the brain. This was a man not to be taken lightly.

Adler looked up, saying, "I'm quite busy, what is it you want, young man? Get on with your business, please."

"Mr. Adler, I am Shannon Murphy from the Smoky Mountains, and I need your help. Let me explain, sir," Shannon said.

Shannon instinctively trusted the man and related the more important events from the time he left the Smokies until arriving in Louisville. Mr. Adler didn't strike Shannon as one who would listen to a long tale of woe, so he stuck to the bare bone facts, making it as brief as possible. He ended by dumping his pouch of gold coins on the desk between them.

"I'm hungry, and I need some trappings," Shannon explained. "I don't want to lose or squander my inheritance for it would mightily disappoint Ma and Pa. Plus, there's the fact that I want desperately to move out West and find a life of my own.

When Adler saw the pile of gold coins on his desk, he looked up in amazement. In a shocked, almost reverent voice, he said, "Young man, I have owned and sold many a rare coin in my businesses over the years but none so fine as these. They are part of the lost crown of wealth of a certain king of England. Such coins as these are more valuable than you can imagine and have brought death to more than one person. What would you have me do with them?"

"It would pleasure me if you could sell them and put the money on deposit with your bank. Pa once told us one of his ancestors, in the old country, stumbled on a great hidden treasure. Perhaps that's where they came from," Shannon added.

Mr. Adler pulled a cord and as the sound of the bell faded a man entered the room. He stood at attention before the desk. "Mr. George, make an accounting of these coins. List each separately with full description. But, before you do, bring a hundred dollars in smaller coin and letters of recommendation from our company to the following merchants," Mr. Adler ordered. He wrote out the list and handed it across the desk.

Looking up at Shannon he continued speaking, "Within three days you will have an accounting on the worth and sale of the coins. Once accomplished, you may place your money on deposit with our bank, or if you desire to do so, you many buy shares in our various business ventures such as the river trade from here to New Orleans. There also is the freighting venture to the far west, which is highly lucrative yet extremely hazardous."

Without hesitation Shannon requested one fourth of his money be invested in the business of shipping and freighting. If he had all that much money, certainly it would not be foolish to risk a dab here and there. As he sat there chewing on the investment idea, a question kept rising in his mind.

"Does Mr. Samuels invest in your shares?" Shannon asked.

"Indeed, he does and has had for many years. In fact, at the present time he is a fairly wealthy man as a result of it," Mr. Adler said.

Shannon considered the reply for a moment or two. If investment with Adler was good enough for Mr. Samuels, it ought to be good enough for him. He decided to up his ante in the game of commerce.

"Mr. Adler, if you don't mind, change the numbers and split my money half and half," Shannon requested.

"Well done, Mr. Murphy. I'll see that your instructions are carried out immediately. In the meantime, go to the hotel on the corner of Fourth and Broadway. Give this note to the desk clerk. One of my assistants will see that appropriate clothing is sent to your room. I should like it if you would join my party in the dining room promptly at seven o'clock," Mr. Adler replied.

As Shannon walked out the door he said to himself, *That must have been a gosh awful lot of money I dumped on Mr. Adler's desk. Why, here I am a bit shy of full manhood, being treated like a man of means.*

The hotel room was almost as big as Shannon's birthing cabin. There was an indoor outhouse with a huge copper tub filled with steaming hot water. On the bed clothes were laid out; light gray shirt, black trousers, short black jacket, underwear, socks, belt, and boots. Standing before a mirror fully clothed presented Shannon with the image of a stranger. As a matter of fact he had never stood in front of a big mirror before in his life. He had only seen his face in Aenid's mirror.

A shock of unruly curly black hair capped his head. Below was a walnut brown face. Endless days in the wild, of rugged travel, buffeted by wind and sun, had darkened the skin. Broad shoulders filled the shirt. The pants were too large for his slim waist but the legs, cut slender, stretched tightly over the bulging muscles of his thighs created by weeks of walking from morning until night from the Smokies to Ohio. Steel gray eyes with pinpoints of fire stared back at him with mysteriously strange, almost devil-may-care, appearance. At that very moment he felt the presence of his ma and pa and the rustle of spirits within. This was a presence that never left Shannon. From that moment on he called it the present past.

The dining room was crowded. A waiter stepped to Shannon's side, leading the way to a quiet alcove table. Others had already been seated. Mr. Adler stood and introduced him to a Mr. Brown and a Mr. Cook. From that point on the evening was long on talk but short on food; that is, as far as Shannon was concerned. The first he enjoyed, the latter he endured.

Before him was a plate of small slimy gray things cupped in what looked like rocks. "Oysters," Mr. Adler said.

"Never," Shannon said. Shannon watched flabbergasted as they took them up an slurped them down with great relish. Then there were chunks of beef called steaks. When Shannon cut into his, it was bloody, absolutely raw. Why, back home he had seen cows hurt no worse than that by a cougar get well.

They may have shorted him on food but the conversation was mind filling. In the hills when the elders gathered to talk, the younguns sat by with mouths closed and ears open. Those elders were pretty smart. They talked from the book of life crammed with every kind of happening and goings-on. Every listening mountain child learned how a spider's web packed on a wound would stop bleeding, what roots and herbs were beneficial, how to steal honey from a bee tree without being stung, and what a body used to treat a sick animal. There was a whole world filled with knowledge for those who would only listen and learn. Shannon learned early in life that if one added two parts of learning by word of mouth with two parts book learning, then topped that off with about ten parts of common sense, one could become right knowledgeable. It was unbelieving what a fellow could learn by listening, reading, and mulling things over.

And Shannon did, especially of the money to be made in the river cargo trade. Moving down the Ohio and into the Mississippi was an endless stream of highly lucrative commerce.

It startled Shannon when Mr. Adler abruptly turned and directed an inquiry to him.

"Shannon, what are your plans for the future?" Mr. Adler asked.

"I don't rightly know at the moment, but for starters that flat and keelboat business sounds mighty interesting. Yes, indeed, mighty interesting," Shannon replied.

"We have a keelboat and a flatboat leaving Louisville this week, Shannon, and the crew is one short. You have a job if you want it. You would work the barge going down and the keel boat coming back up. If you join the crew, I warn you the work will be hard, but if you invest in the cargo you will get a share of the profits. Of course you will receive the normal wages of thirty dollars a month," Mr. Adler offered.

"Who's head of the crew?" Shannon asked.

"Captain Gillis is in charge. He's as tough as dried buffalo hide and as crusty as an alkali pan. He'll treat you fairly. Learn as much as you can from him and his crew. They are a cut above most that's on the river. The fare will be plain and plentiful. Work will be nonstop and you sleep when you can. You'll be fighting the elements, bugs, beasts, and two-legged varmints, both red and white. But all of that will help make you a man," Mr. Adler said.

Now, that last bit about helping make Shannon a man was more than a bit irksome. He did, however, let it pass without reply.

"Just tell me when and where I am to meet Captain Gillis and I'll be on my way. First though, I want to speak my thankfuls to all of you. Kindness has been hard to come by since leaving the hills. We mountain folk ain't a bunch of forgetfuls. If any of you need something, just speak my name and I'll come a running. It ain't likely that people such as you would need my help but know for certain that such as it is, is yours," Shannon said.

Shannon's words were sincere and they knew it, yet they did seem a bit surprised. Mr. Brown winked at Mr. Adler, speaking to Shannon as he turned his head, "Young man, take care. On your return you may be surprised by a proposed new venture. But discussion of that can await your return."

From time to time over the next several months Shannon thought on what Mr. Brown had said and wondered what kind of proposition he had in mind.

From the moment the lines were slipped and the portage of the Falls of the Ohio had faded from view to the end of the journey to New Orleans, it was nothing but work from eyelid open to eyelid shut. And at times it was from can't see to can see. The flatboat was filled with barrel after barrel of fine Kentucky sour mash whiskey. There was no more highly prized or sought after commodity anywhere along the river. Movement was slow. The only speed was that of the river's flow. Days seemed long and nights without end.

Nights were the worst. To sleep below deck in an effort to escape the insects was to be stifled by heat and humidity. To sleep on deck was to be constantly drained of blood by mosquitoes. Gnats and mosquitoes came not in swarms but in clouds. Out would come the smudge pots producing billows of black oily smoke. It was hard to tell which created the greater discomfort, the insects or the smudge pots. One drank your blood; the other chocked your lungs.

From time to time the monotony of the trip was broken by anticipated as well as unexpected events. If the humdrums really settled in on the crew and raw edges of ill temper surfaced, Captain Gillis would tap one of the barrels of whiskey and give the men time to vent their spleens. As often as not, rough housing would start and river boatmen wrestling would become a serious business. Among the Cherokees wrestling was a refined art, so Shannon joined in the sport, naively feeling he had a decided edge. It took the crew little more than a heartbeat to blunt that edge.

What a choice crew it was. Rom was a Romanian gypsy from central Europe who spoke a half-dozen languages well and could curse in the rest of them. One could easily tell that Waldroop, the Englishman, was a man of cultural refinement yet used the language and possessed the manner of a frontier boatman. Stellwagen, on the other hand, was something of a mystery. He possessed a military bearing, and his rigidly disciplined lifestyle often alienated those about him. Every once in a while there would be a slight show of arrogance or smug superiority by Stellwagen but for this he would apologize.

On the slow trip down the river Shannon began to learn more and more about the crew. At a stopover, as the flatboat was being nudged toward a landing, a huge cottonmouth moccasin dropped from an overhanging limb to the deck of the boat. It barely started moving when the whisper of the sound passed by Shannon's shoulder and the snake was pinned to the boat deck. A silent messenger of death, a thin-bladed stiletto, quivered as the snake thrashed about. Looking back he saw Rom standing on top of the cabin with a broad grin on his face. He said, "Some things seem to be about as swift as the strike of a snake. What do you say my young friend?" With an almost inaudible voice to the swiftness of what had happened Shannon replied with a question, "Rom, is this some kind of gypsy magic? I've never seen you with a knife in the weeks we have been together. Where did it come from?"

Boys growing up always threw things. In the mountains they threw knives and hatchets, even axes, always trying to perfect the art and be one who could hit the mark. Shannon's skills with knife and tomahawk were fair but nothing like those of Rom. How could anyone so miraculously cause a knife to appear, much less throw it with such deadly accuracy?

That night Rom became Shannon's teacher. In the following weeks he learned tricks of knife fighting he didn't know existed. It was from Rom that he became aware of the fact that knife fighting was an art among gypsies with many of it secrets passed from one generation to the next. From him Shannon learned the stance, the pivot, the positioning of the knife in hand, the thrust, and the parry as in fencing, the blurred movement of the hand to fool the opponent's eye, the fake and thrust, and the vulnerable spots on hand, wrist, arm, neck, thigh, and ankle, which could render an opponent virtually helpless.

Nor did he fail to teach Shannon the importance of the weapon itself and the way it was carried. No blades were better forged or balanced than those produced by gypsy smiths. From India they derived methods of producing a special steel, to this was added refinement of Toledo blade making acquired during gypsy rovings through Spain. From the Moors of Spain they learned the craft of producing Damascus steel by forging layers of metal together. Such blades were of superb strength and held the keenest of edges. Its sheath was hung by a thong around the neck hidden beneath the shirt or tunic. To own and master the use of such a weapon was one of Shannon's dreams, and master it he did. Rom had never had such an apt student as Shannon. His reflexes were not those of a growing boy but those of an accomplished fencer.

One late evening Stellwagen and Shannon were sitting on the cabin top. A stiff breeze had driven the insects away. For a long while there was silence. Then Stellwagen began to share with him something of his past. He was from an aristocratic Prussian military family but had to flee Europe after a duel. He had killed the husband of the woman with whom he was having an affair.

They had a saying back in the hollows that stealing the goose's first egg is the hardest, the rest come easier. That was the way things went in the relationship between Shannon and Stellwagen. Once Stellwagen started talking there came long sessions of sharing. It was apparent that Stellwagen had long awaited one such as Shannon, who would listen with appreciation about that which had consumed his former life. Most military men were reticent when it came to telling the stories of combat. That is quite true if the occasion is casual conversation. For one who had been a ranking officer, however, the opportunity to share the critical information on tactics and logistics with an ardent young learner was considered to be a gift.

Stellwagen from the moment he set eyes on Shannon felt a strong attachment to him. Early in the relationship he decided to share such knowledge as he had, which would assist him in meeting the rigid demands of those who would seek to forge a new way of life in a raw frontier.

He shared account after account of battles and their strategy, the effectiveness of guerilla warfare, hit-and-run tactics of the American Indians, and Napoleon's artillery genius.

Nor was Waldroop reluctant to share with Shannon from his past. It provided him with invaluable information. He taxed Shannon's brain with endless lectures on English common laws, finally revealing a well-hidden secret. He had abandoned his former profession as a solicitor when he failed to become a barrister. Disapproval in him by his family, who for a hundred years had been barristers and judges of the queen's court, were vocalized at every family gathering. After one particular bitter family squabble, Waldroop packed a few of his personal items and a box of books. After with drawing his meager savings from a local bank, booked passage on a ship to New Orleans. Six months later he was a keelboat man.

For the first time Shannon was coming to grips with a totally new view of the westward expansion. Cities of the East were melting pots of ethnic groups and cultures with each seeking their future and fortune. At the same time they sought to maintain their identity involved in the surging western migration; background was discarded to create what was to be "westerner." It was a new creature formed of people of all nations, languages, cultures, offsprings of the times, and products of a new world and way of existence. They all stood on the same level. It was a breed of man never before seen, spawn of their environment. It mattered not who or what one had been but whether they could meet the challenges offered. Loyalty, discipline, courage, honor, frankness, sincerity, and honesty were coin of the realm. The game was played on the field of personal integrity. This was at once Shannon's challenge and task. Did he have what it took to get the coon? as the saying went back in the hills. Time only would tell.

Hours turned into endless days and days turned into limitless weeks. Time seemed to disappear and Shannon's world was filled with struggle against the river. Flatboats were unwieldy at their best and brutal to control. Wind and current fought with diabolical force the hand at the steering sweeps. At times he bitterly complained as some sudden swirl of current or rush of fresh breeze nearly wrenched the sweep arm from his hands, only to hear the sarcastic rejoinder of Rom, "Cheer up, little one, it's nothing but a bit of wind and a trickle of water. It was the "little one" bit that ticked Shannon off. Rom was five-eight, he was almost six-three and growing.

During the trip down river, Stellwagen had shocked Shannon with the statement: "At New Orleans we deliver the cargo. Then the flatboat will be dismantled and sold for lumber or possibly firewood for sternwheelers. Then we keelboat back. That's when we'll separate the boys from the men. You haven't seen hard until we make the trip back."

How a boat could be moved upstream against the mighty Mississippi was a puzzle. The answer, when it came, brought nothing but backbreaking work. How right Stellwagen had been!

On the trip down river Shannon had seen a host of keelboats close inshore being poled at a snail's pace against the current. At other times long tow lines snaked out from the bow of the boats and pulled taunt by crews who trudged along the shore, moving the heavy vessels against the current. Shannon didn't shun work and was more than willing to do his share, but moving a keelboat upstream against the oncoming flow looked to him like a man trying to roll a huge boulder, much too heavy for him, up a mountain pass.

Everything about the river threatened the flatboat and its crew. Swirling currents produced whirlpools, which in turn sought to violently whip the tiller in a manner that would throw a body overboard. Constantly shifting sand bars and deceptively shallow underwater mud banks reached out to suck luckless crafts into their clutches. Virtually invisible snags, at times whole trees carried by spring floods and imbedded in the shallow bottom, reared their deadly bobbing heads like monstrous serpents ready to pierce the hull. Swift moving thunderstorms sent impenetrable curtains of rain that obscured the shoreline and caused the flatboat to move in sightless danger.

Down the Ohio and into the Mississippi near Cairo the flatboat moved. Memphis and Jackson were passed and finally New Orleans was in view. Shannon had survived it all and was none the worse from wear. But New Orleans itself posed a different threat to Shannon.

The view that greeted Shannon staggered his imagination. Stretching before his eyes was a levy some five miles long jammed with vessels of every type and size. There were high masted ships of almost every nation involved in maritime trade, river sternwheelers, coastal schooners, barges, and keelboats without number. Along the waterfront docks, some two hundred feet long, thousands of laborers moved merchandise from vessel to warehouse and from warehouse to vessel. New Orleans was the destination and the distribution point of goods from the entire Ohio Valley. No greater international marketplace existed in the United States at that time.

His friends had drunk out in three days. Shannon had no love for partying city life. The hustle, noise, and confusion caused him to long for the high "lonesomes." On landing he learned that the war had ended weeks previously. As a result, a city noted for its gaiety was somewhat restrained and solemn. Concerned talk was everywhere about the occupation of the city by Federal troops.

Months later Shannon heard of the looting of New Orleans by a Union colonel who commanded the occupation forces. He had amassed a fortune by confiscating the possessions of the wealthy. It was common knowledge he was British and during the war had served in the Union intelligence, trying to identify any British suppliers of war material to the South. Specifically his agents were to ferret out the times and routes of shipments from England so they could be intercepted by the Federal navy. It takes a man of mighty low principles to betray his own. Only once did Shannon hear a description of the man, never his name. Something about talk of the man nagged at the edges of Shannon's memory, but he couldn't fill in the blank spaces.

One event which occurred on Shannon's first night in New Orleans caused him hours of introspection. No happening since his ma and pa's death prompted so much thought.

No high country boy, recently uprooted from the hills, was ready for such an elegant dining experience. The hotel dining room was as large as an oak grove. Shannon had never seen so many tables covered with white sheets. There appeared to be enough knives, forks, and spoons for a family at each place. In front of the plates were folded snow-white napkins. There were all sorts of drinking glasses of different sizes and flowers in a bowl.

After being seated a man approached Shannon in what he took to be a funeral outfit and asked, "Sir, would you like a menu?" Now that one threw him. If it was something to eat, it didn't sound too good. Remembering the oysters back in Louisville, Shannon answered, "Mister, I'm a plain mountain boy who came down the river from Louisville on a flatboat. I don't know what a menu is or whether you should shoot it or run from it. One thing I do know for certain, I'm about starved out and in need of food and a whole lot of that." A toothsome smile broke out across the waiter's face who laughingly said, "At last an honest man without pretense. I, Louie, will see that you are fed."

Shannon didn't know what gumbo was, and when he finished eating still didn't know what it was. Never had he tasted anything so good. The fourth bowl ladled over a bed of snow-white rice was before him when it happened.

The dining room was filled. People were at every table and most of them dressed sort of dandified. One man suddenly jumped upright, turning his chair over. Clutched in his hand was a napkin. Without so much as a by-your-leave he slashed the face of the man across the table from him with the napkin. Slowly the man who had been struck rose from his seat and said in a hissing whisper, "I demand satisfaction here and now."

Back in the hills a person would have just reached over, jerked him across the table by the throat and backhanded him so hard he would have heard dogs chasing a coon.

They, however, immediately left the hotel. Shannon followed. In the rear of the hotel was a garden square. He finally pushed his way to where he could see the two men, each with pistol in hand, standing back to back. On command they walked ten paces and again on command turned and fired. Both were hit and hit hard; one in the chest, the other in the stomach. A duel face-to-face either took a lot of courage or a passel of blatant stupidity. Shannon could not help but wonder if he had the nerve, the iron discipline it would take to look at the muzzle of a gun, knowing it was kill or be killed. On the way up the Mississippi he would think on that many times.

Before leaving New Orleans, word came from Mr. Adler, as well as Brown and Cook, inviting Shannon to join a train of freighters out of St. Joe headed for the far West. Complete instructions would await him in St. Joe. Nothing could have pleased him more. Memories of the tales told by his pa, and his dreams of someday going west, were ever with Shannon whose head was filled with the stories of mountain men and their exploits. Someway he felt deep down inside that his future lay in the direction. Adler and Brown had long discussed that night in Louisville the growing demand for beef in the West and how fortunes would be made in that business. An idea began to form in Shannon's mind at that time. Could he build a cattle ranch in the valley of his dreams?

The trip down river was child's play compared to the return. The incessant walking of the pole men, from bow to stern was relentless. On either side of the deck, in tandem, the pole men moved along the narrow ledge between cabin and rail. Underfoot were smoothly worn cleats nailed to the deck to give greater traction as the boat was pushed. By keeping simultaneous pace and pole pressure the craft crept along through the shallow water near the banks. Hands became callused and hard, thigh and calf muscles bulged, shoulders broadened, wrists thickened, and biceps ached and grew. At night, spasms of pain would rouse Shannon from the deepest sleep as muscles knotted. Hands were the worst. Calluses thickened and dried then split open, bleeding. Lard from the stores was worked into the iron-like flesh to soften the insensitive skin. It was to no avail for the next day it was back to the poles or towing ropes.

After two months on the river Shannon finally arrived at St. Joe a vastly different person. Mind and body had been transformed. Stellwagen had introduced him to the military tactics and drilled him in their use. Other hours were spent with Rom, exhausting Shannon to the point of collapse. Practice with the knife and the caveat, after grueling hours at the poles, left him spent but stronger, more agile and deadlier as an opponent in any combat. It was Waldroop, however, who challenged his thinking, probed his logical reasoning, and caused him to recognize the power of the law to govern the conduct of men in humane society. Where there was no law, men did what was right in their own eyes. Each was judge, jury, and executioner. Waldroop totally surprised Shannon during one discussion when he said, "Shannon, I'm not a very religious man, but I am beginning to believe that no person can keep the law of the land unless he can keep the basic rules of conduct found in religion. Not only do my rights stop where your rights begin, but I must protect your rights as I protect my own."

Never had the three teachers chanced upon a more eager student. Shannon, never before challenged in intellectual pursuits, became insatiable in his quest for more knowledge. His quick, inquiring mind had leapt to the invitation of learning. "Anything learned is never a waste," Rom would say with a twinkle in his eyes. All Shannon had learned would at one time or another find a place of value in his life.

CHAPTER 3

Freighting Days

St. Joe teemed with life. Everywhere people milled about, and when they moved it was at a hurried pace. On the outskirts, and into the town, immigrant wagons, freight wagons, newly built Conestoga wagons moved in endless procession. Wagons too slight to attempt the arduous westward journey were abandoned but were swiftly stripped of tongues, wheels, planking, and hardware for use as temporary repairs for buckboards, buggies, and carts. An electric excitement filled the air. Everywhere there was bartering for needed supplies, brawling in the streets and saloons, and hawkers vending their wares. In the midst of such chaos, wagon train leaders and freight masters desperately sought to form into some semblance of order the trains, which biweekly departed for the West.

Written on the faces of the people were bright hopes born of dreams. Many saw the open West's door as a way out of the squalor of eastern city life. Others saw it as an escape from social or economic oppression. Multitudes felt it to be the fulfillment of cherished dreams to work soil that was theirs and rear children in freedom from the tyranny of a landed gentry.

For the defeated secessionists the way was open to start afresh. Behind them were the shambles of a way of life that could never be revived. The winds of change were sweeping across the land and with it the challenge to become part of the making of a new nation.

On the other hand there were legions of corrupt malcontents. They were the dregs of a wartime winnowing, nothing more than leeches who fed upon the disadvantaged and weak. They were the users and the takers. Yet among them were those who rose to the top of the seething caldron of opportunists. Those of political power and wealth, hungry for more, were the most malignant.

They were the proud, arrogant, powerful railroad and cattle barons intent upon control of land for grazing or right-of-ways. While one claimed all the free range the others claimed hundreds of thousands of acres by federal grant as railroad right-of-ways. Thousands upon thousands of excess acres in the hands of railroad moguls would be sold to those seeking land to farm. Men of lesser power who stood in their way were crushed. It was a time and place of violence and gun law.

As Shannon reflected on what he had seen and heard, it began to dawn on him that this was more than just a simple westward movement of people. It was the forging of a new nation out of dreams anticipated or dreams destroyed. This was the creating of that country envisioned by the founding fathers. A place where the meaning of individual worth and inherent dignity of each person would ultimately find fulfillment.

Moving along the crowded streets Shannon made his way to the offices of L.& P. Express Co. There he was welcomed by the manager. Already, they had received word of his coming from Adler and Co. He was given the name of a hotel and instructions on making connections with their freight train leaving Leavenworth for the far West only a week hence. As he left he wondered why the manager looked at him in such a quizzical manner. It seemed the whole time they talked his face was marked with suppressed laughter.

On the way to the hotel, Shannon was shocked by his image reflected in a shop window. It was a vastly different image than that seen a month previously in Louisville. His clothing was ill fitting to say the least. The cuffs of his shirt rose well above his wrist, and his pants legs were above his ankles. Shirt seams were strained and broken at points due to broadening shoulders. His pants' waist was gathered into a fold by his belt and the seat baggy. A bronzed face and shock of sun-faded hair stared at him. Shannon grinned and said to himself, *If first impressions are important, then I am a miserable failure.* No wonder the employees of L & P Express had looked on him with some curiosity! He decided, however, to wait until arriving at Leavenworth to outfit himself. In the streets there were more than a few dressed as he was.

For well over two decades Adler and Co. had been factors for a vast western freighting enterprise. Tandem wagons drawn by ten to twelve oxen or mules, carrying eight to ten thousand pounds of freight crossed plains and high mountains. Before the coming of railroads, and for some time afterward, they were the lifeline of the West. Life was made a bit more tolerable on the frontier as a result of their presence. A far-flung chain of army posts, mining camps, and small towns depended upon this risky but lucrative business. After the advent of railroads, out of way, noncentral towns were served by companies such as M. Carroll and Co., Garrison and Wyatt Co., and Diamond R or Overland Freight Line.

Since Shannon was an investor with Adler and Co., who acted on behalf of and transacted business for L. & P. Freight Co., he was immediately signed on as an assistant scout under the tutelage of Beckworth, called Beck for short, L. & P.'s chief wagon master and scout. He was assigned to the next train leaving in one week from Leavenworth, the staging depot for L. & P. The final destinations of the train were Fort Kearney and Fort Laramie. Nothing could have pleased Shannon more. It brought him closer to that dreamed-of high mountain country and the valley of his hopes and dreams.

Within the week Shannon was in Leavenworth. Fort Leavenworth, the post that opened the West, was located on the bluffs of the Missouri River. It had become the base of army operations to protect the westward expansion of the nation. Shortly after its establishment it became the gateway to the Oregon and Santa Fe Trails, as well as the point of resupply for army posts strung across the frontier all the way to California.

Everywhere Shannon looked he saw the blue-shirted soldiers of the First Dragoons, Company B. Beck told him they were the only soldiers permitted to wear shirts rather than tunics due to the intense prairie heat.

With Beck's help Shannon went about the business of outfitting himself for the trip ahead.

The process of obtaining necessities was a revelation to Shannon. Of the end of available merchandise there was no sight. Leavenworth was like a monstrous funnel that gathered into itself the thousands moving westward, civilian and military. It then spewed them out in a steady stream of horses and Conestoga wagons, oxen and freight wagons, cavalry and foot soldiers.

Only two stops were required to obtain everything on the spartan list Beck had given Shannon. He was instructed to buy only those personal items, which could be packed in his saddle bags and blanket roll. Everything else would be transported in supply wagons.

Shannon, since leaving the Smokies, had kept his possibles bag close at hand for it was his survival kit. He would add one change of clothes then make the additional purchases Beck insisted upon. He was a no-nonsense man when it came to following his suggestions. On the corner of Fifth and Delaware streets was a huge hardware and a few steps up the street was Smith and Co. mercantile. Shannon was shocked at the prices. *Why,* he thought to himself, *who's ever heard of sixty cents for a pair of riveted sailcloth Levi's or twenty cents for a shirt!*

At the hardware Shannon laid his old Colt Navy .36 on the counter along with his Henry rifle. These were traded in for a new .44 Colt Army and a newer model .44 Henry and six boxes of shells. Beckworth had convinced him of the importance of having rifle and six-gun in the same caliber so the shells could be used interchangeably. Although Beck still kept an 1849 Colt Pocket pistol in his saddlebags, he insisted that the newer Colts were more reliable and greatly decreased reloading time.

To this point in time Shannon had not been a horseman. For the rest of his life, however, he would be viewing the world from a horse's back. Saddle, tack, blanket roll, and saddlebags, as well as horses, were to be purchased. Shannon hated to admit it but decisions on how and what to buy were beyond him.

He approached Beck, saying, "I've got eighty dollars in gold and a letter of credit from Adler and Co. You tell me I need a bridle, saddle, holster, lariat, and saddle blanket, which I don't know anything about. You also tell me I need two good horses."

"That's right, Shannon, and you need to make the purchases today. Get accustomed to your saddle and mounts as quickly as possible. By the way, you'll find breaking in a saddle like sitting on a cactus pad," Beck replied.

"Beck, I'd be skinned alive in a horse trade. I'm plumb ignorant about such," Shannon added.

Beck smiled, saying, "Shannon, it takes a smart man to admit his limitations. I'll be right proud to help you."

A few hours later Shannon had his horses and a working man's saddle. Within those few hectic days before leaving Leavenworth, Beck and Shannon began to feel a strong bond growing between them. Each sensed within the other something of themselves: a hidden strength, an intensity of purpose, a hardened and disciplined will, a self-assurance without swagger or elevated ego, and a shared love for taxing physical work. Each reveled at the challenge presented to anyone who sought a new way of life, which at every turn found barriers created by man and nature. Beck faced them with the experience and wisdom of years. Shannon faced them with a youthful exuberance tempered with insights well beyond his age and a willingness to learn.

Daily Beck and Shannon scouted ahead of the train but never so far they could not quickly return in case of need. On such an occasion Beck, half-turned in his saddle, asked, "Why westward, Shannon?"

"To tell you the truth, I do and I don't know," Shannon replied. "I can't tell if I am chasing my own dream or that of Pa's. He always had a yen to go find a certain hidden valley in the land of Cheyenne spoken of by mountain men. Irish Murphy, his grandfather, had lived over a year there in the 1840s. It is a high valley in the land of the northern Cheyenne. I'll know it when I find it. Sometimes I feel I am a bit shy of a full load of corn, because at night I seem to hear from time to time a voice in a dream telling me to come. The speaker is a shadowy figure in the clothing of a mountain man. He is standing in a high gap looking down on a valley fed by two tumbling streams." Then Shannon added, "Now I have a question for you. Why did I see, back in Leavenworth, some freight wagons being harnessed to mules rather than hooked to oxen?"

"Given the right breaks in the weather, mule trains travel at a faster pace than oxen," Beck replied. "When supplies are sorely needed, or when resupplying forts become critical prior to the onset of late autumn and winter storms, mules are used. Mule- or horse-drawn wagons, however, are utilized at all times of the year. There are a lot of independents, short-haul freighters, who totally depend on mules."

A few days later, Shannon, riding slightly ahead of Beck, topped a slight rise. In the swale below he saw a small herd of antelope. Whipping his rifle from the scabbard Shannon fired two swift shots, jacking the shells with practiced ease. One antelope was hit with the first steps of flight; the second was dropped not more than thirty yards from where it had been grazing. Beck, who had never seen Shannon shoot, was silent for a moment before saying with a pleased look on his face, "You're a bit sudden, aren't you? That was a fine piece of shooting at over a hundred yards. Hunted much?"

"Growing up, Pa allowed how I could shoot all I wanted as long as meat was fetched with each shot. I durn near wore out a little Lancaster Pennsylvania squirrel rifle on everything from boomers to deer. If it was to be toted or dragged I got it with that gun."

As the days turned into weeks Shannon slowly learned more and more about Beck. It was not that Beck shunned conversation, rather he was completely immersed in his responsibilities as the wagon master. From saddle on to saddle off, Beck went about his task, giving his attention to the smallest detail. Even when scouting ahead of the train with Shannon, jawing was seldom. When asked about this by Shannon, the reply was a lesson in common sense spoken in a gravelly voice.

"Talk can get you killed, and that right sudden! When you palaver with someone, you are listening to them in order to catch what they're saying. If you listen proper, like you look your man in the eye, you read his face and connect it with the words. It just isn't proper not to pay attention or miss the meaning of what they are saying. Yet when you do, you shut out the whole world around you, which might be trying to tell you something important. That something could threaten this train, even be the death of us all. Take Indians, for example. They ride in silence, never taking their eyes off their surroundings. They stay alert to any possible danger. Save your small talk for the camp at night or when you sit your horse with plenty of cover and broad range of view. If there is nothing moving and only nature's sounds coming your way then speak your piece, but do it softly and briefly."

Thus, it was from Beck that Shannon learned the language and lessons of the plains and western mountains.

"Shannon," Beck started, "nature is constantly speaking her native language. All senses have to be attuned to her tongue. She communicates with every sense that we have. Seeing, hearing, touching, and smelling have to be developed to a point of alertness and perception by any would-be plainsmen or mountain man. Such is completely alien to the uninitiated. Each communication has its peculiar and sometimes puzzling meaning. It all needs to be filtered through your senses and responded to without delay.

"Smoke seen or smelled when anticipated is one thing; where unexpected, another. Distant swirls of dust, or even just a wisp of it in the air or the smell of it on the calm night air, have to be translated into understandable terms. Was it a distant dust devil? In what direction did it seem to be moving? From its size, direction, and thickness the wilderness intruder has to determine whether it is stampeding wild horses, buffalo on the move, or an Indian war party. Should a rabbit bolt from its hiding place, a grouse explode into sudden flight, a spooked deer snort, a marmot give a shrill warning whistle, what does it mean? Sky, earth, wind, and creatures of nature are all textbooks to be read from, their lessons learned."

Beck was speaking of survival and Shannon gave his words rapt attention as he continued, "Yet the hardest lesson of all to master by the white man in the West is that of patience and stillness. When a person has developed enough self-discipline to remain immobile for hours, without food, drink, or a smoke, then they are well on their way to surviving the dangers of the West.

"Gun savvy is important as well as dress. Clothing and horses, whose colors blend with the buff hues of sand and rock merging with the greens and brown of the forest and prairie, are virtually invisible when frozen in stillness."

Shannon was daily adding new lessons to the old—those learned during growing up time in the Smokies.

Beck was the instructor, Shannon the student. It was the ideal learning situation, one-on-one. The learning of years began to flow from Beck to Shannon— information self-gained or garnered from acquaintances, friends, or family.

It was rumored that Beck was the grandson of James Beckworth, one of the greatest of the mountain men, and an Indian wife. As Shannon thought on this, he realized how fortunate it was to be thrown into the company of such a man. Frontier ken was a thing to be shared, not kept to one's self. The passing on of such knowledge, gained by firsthand experience was a major factor in the success of many, such as Shannon, who moved west. With it they were much better suited to turn an untamed land into cattle ranches to feed a hungry postwar nation. Physical threats were one thing. Another was the emotional threats of a land that fostered a sense of loneliness, isolation, down right inhospitable climate and awesome endlessness. The latter could be more deadly than the former.

The country's expanse, seas of tall grass rolling in undulating waves like an ocean, stretched to the far horizons. Many were intimidated by its sheer vastness; others cowered and threatened, overawed by its unbroken nothingness. Would-be settlers were forced to face their littleness in comparison to the immensity of the plains and the horrendous forces of nature, which hovered about as some gigantic nemesis. Nature's capricious whims, when suddenly unleashed upon emigrant trains, freighters, cattle drovers or lone movers, were enough to try the souls of the hardiest.

Across the plains swept swift, unexpected, and violent storms. In late spring or early autumn, howling blizzards periodically struck with slashing, cutting, icy snow as fine as hominy grits. Snow might also come as a blanket of huge soft flakes blotting out the sky above and the land below. The northern plains, foothills, and high mountains could quickly become a silent frozen world threatening all life. At other times devastating winds raced over the prairie with a sound like that of stampeding buffalo. From foreboding clouds a black swirling funnel often twisted its devastating path across the expanse. Anything and everything before it was destroyed. From time to time the whole landscape was lashed by driving rain or ravaged by wild fires, which sprang up as a result of lightning strikes on sun-bleached grass. In the face of such calamities many a weary sojourner to the western lands was broken in spirit. Their dreams turned to dust. Abandoning all, they returned East despondent and virtually penniless. The West was settled by sheer perseverance in the face of constant danger.

As they rode, Beck's eyes never left the far expanses or immediate surroundings. Whenever he stepped from the saddle it was carbine in hand.

Shannon was quick to observe that Beck kept his right hand free and empty whenever possible.

"Beck, why do you habitually try to keep your right hand empty?" Shannon asked. "I've watched you swing a pick and an axe. About every other swing you sorta' straighten up, holding the handle in your left hand and quickly scan the area."

"Let me tell you a brief story, Shannon," Beck replied. "For many years I have been one of the fastest and most accurate gunhands around. That's no brag, just plain simple truth. For a while I rode shotgun for Butterfield and Butterfield stagecoach lines and never lost a strong box. I've served some time with the Texas Rangers and did a stint as a deputy marshal. In my day, I've had to kill my man, but not of my own doing. I never hauled iron unless forced to do so. Behind me is a string of would-be gunslicks who would like nothing better than to plant me in some lonely grave or town boot hill. I've stayed alive being ready to face any gun challenge or other danger coming on me. I want that right hand free 'cause you can't tell when one of them polecats is going to have at you."

Shannon thought to himself, *This is another bit of wisdom to mull over.*

Bullwhackers and muleteers were paid thirty dollars and didins per month, while freight masters were paid the handsome sum of one hundred twenty-five dollars. Only the toughest, wariest, steady, and skilled man could handle the job. Knowledge of stock, the land, and men was a must, as well as a sixth sense to anticipate trouble. Bullwhackers and muleteers were difficult to control and the trail boss had to be one who commanded respect, even if grudgingly. Beck was such a man.

No life was rougher than that of the muleteers or bullwhackers of freight trains. The standard of living was a step lower than that of a dog's life without home or master. Living conditions were spartan. There was an abundance of food such as it was: coffee, sourdough bread, sow-belly fried, and gravy made from the grease. Occasionally wild onions and fortunately found herbs were a welcomed addition to the diet.

There were, however, those rare freight companies who provided better fare—L. & P. was one of them. Rations included beef, flour, bacon, coffee, beans or potatoes, dried fruit, salt, soap, and soda[2]—all shared in the common day of backbreaking, physically exhausting, work. While the muleskinner rode on the wagon, guiding and controlling the team with a "jerk" line, the bullwhacker

---

[2]   Recorded in Ashby, "Rules and Regulations for Freighting"

walked by the front wheels of the wagon. From there he stopped, turned or urged on teams of four to six yoke of oxen with a swirling, cracking whip with which he could draw blood at thirty feet. No harder drinking, odious of body and mouth, or belligerent group of men were to be found in the West. Many were army deserters from the cavalry outposts of the western command or "galvanized Yankees." These were Confederates, formerly Union prisoners, who were released after taking an oath that they would not return to the Confederate forces and bear arms against the North.

Shannon quickly learned that such men could not be handled with sweet reason. The cock-of-the-walk among the freighters on the trip was "Bull" Harkness. He was, as his nickname, a "bull"—a nasty brute of a man, with disposition to match. The train had pulled into Grinnel to drop off cargo and camp for the night on the outskirts of the village. Grinnel was one of those crossroads towns by a decent spring that had sprung up overnight. Perhaps its chief claim to fame was a bar, the only one for a fifty-mile radius. Over its counter—made of heavy oak planks strapped to barrels—rotgut whisky, which would make a man bark at the moon and chase rabbits, was dispensed.

Harkness, against orders, slipped from the train and within two hours was a roaring whirlwind of destruction in Grinnel's only saloon. By the time word arrived at the camp and Beck entered the saloon with Shannon, the place was in shambles.

"Belly up to the bar, boss," Bull said, "and have yourself a drink or two with me. The Bull is buying."

"Harkness," Beck snapped back with the voice of an Irish drill sergeant, "get yourself back to camp, and do it now!"

Bull turned ugly, saying, "No man talks to Bull that way, especially the mealymouthed son of a squaw woman."

Beck's face turned to stone.

"Bull, step up and take what's coming to you. You need your body scourged and your mind purged. After I've finished the first, if you are still alive, I might attempt the second. When I'm through with you, draw what little pay you have coming after taking care of the damages here, and leave the train for good," Beck retorted.

For his size Bull moved with amazing swiftness. Without warning he was on Beck, swinging sledgehammer fists wildly but effectively. Bull's initial rush caught Beck flatfooted. A thousand shooting stars flared in Beck's head as he slammed against the bar. Bull lunged, with head lowered, to take advantage of his luck. He intended to crush Beck against the bar with the sheer weight of his body. Instead Beck sidestepped and tripped him, battering the bar with Bull's head. Beck backpedaled to gain time to clear his head.

Bull had always depended on his brute strength. He was an above-the-average brawler, but no boxer. Beck moved deceptively. He slipped into a crouch and unleashed two jolting, lightning-fast jabs to the jaw, rocking Bull's head. Then he delivered a hard right to the wind. In the instant before the blow landed, Bull turned slightly to the right and straightened up. Rather than to the wind, the ripping fist went to the kidney. Bull gasped with pain. Beck bored in with a left hook to the jaw and a whistling right to the body. As Bull staggered back, Beck moved in sliding his feet across the floor, keeping his stance solid, and shot a straight right to the jaw. Behind it was the full weight of his body and the strength of his shoulders. It was a classic right punching through and perfectly timed. Bull screamed as his jaw shattered. He then slid to the floor.

Beck turned and headed for the saloon door, thinking Bull was unconscious. Grimacing with pain, Bull pushed himself up on one elbow. From his boot he had drawn a bowie knife. His arm started to whip forward when Shannon happened to glance in that direction. With fluid motion Shannon's gun leapt from leather with dazzling speed. Two shots like rolling thunder filled the room. On either side of the left pocket button on Bull's shirt, holes appeared.

A stunned silence hung over the room. The few witnesses would tell and retell the event. None could say they had actually seen Shannon draw his gun; it was so fast and unanticipated. Yet they testified they saw Bull's arm moving with deadly speed to throw a knife when the shots rang out. He was dead before he could finish the throw. The shooter, Shannon, so they said, was standing by the door; gun palmed with a wisp of smoke rising from its muzzle. Shannon walked over to Beck and said with an even voice as they headed for the door, "You've got to learn something, Beck. Don't ever try to walk away from a rattlesnake until you've cut its head off and buried it deep."

"That's the second time you have taken me completely by surprise, Shannon, with your shooting. You are unbelievably fast and can place your shots. A silver dollar would have covered both. It could be your salvation or your destruction. This I know, I owe you one. You saved my life and that will not be forgotten," Beck replied.

The next day Beck told Shannon that he did not know for certain who his parents were. "One thing," Beck said, "if James Beckworth and an Indian maiden were my parents, I would look on it as an honor. If that was my ancestry, then I couldn't be prouder, and nobody is going to speak slightingly of them."

As the days were on, the train moved slowly toward the northwest, following the Oregon Trail, along a route also used by the Pony Express for its record time of seven days and seventeen hours to carry mail from St. Joe to Sacramento. They had no hint of the danger ahead. No word had reached them of the sudden explosion of raids by the Cheyenne, western Sioux, and Arapaho in the Dakota, Colorado, and Montana territories.

For several days Shannon and Beck had seen tracks of unshod Indian ponies while scouting. They appeared to be nothing more than isolated hunting parties but their proximity to the train resulted in an acute alertness. Additional night guards had been posted, especially to protect the horses. It was said a man could stretch out in the grass on a flat plain with no cover within half a mile to take a nap while holding the reigns of his horse in one hand, only to awake still holding the reins but no horse. Looking about he could see where a Cheyenne had walked away with his mount.

Beck was not greatly disturbed by the presence of the hunting parties. The tracks of no two of the groups of six to eight braves appeared to be heading toward a rendezvous with others to form a war party.

Even the very best could be fooled by the cunning tactics of the Cheyenne. This was precisely what they wanted Beck to think. For days their scouts had been following the train. Each group has approached it from a different direction. They knew of Beck and his Indian blood and saw in him a worthy opponent. When the freighters were deep enough into their territory they would strike. The attack would be typical Cheyenne—swift, overwhelming, and timed to perfection.

They hit the freighter's encampment coming out of the sun as it was rising full over the horizon. Strategy of the Cheyenne was classic. The attack occurred just as the men were rolling out of their blankets and going about early morning tasks. The Indians seemed to materialize like riders coming through shimmering desert heat waves.

One group of the two-pronged assault stampeded the steers. Then they withdrew and joined the major force for a slow, methodical, harassing attack.

The timing of the attack took full advantage of the camp's routine activities of the day. It also demonstrated familiarity with the practices of ox train defenses. Immigrant wagon trains or mule freight trains would circle wagons with the stock tethered close outside the circle, where they were fed with grain, from grain boxes attached to the tailgates of the wagons. Thus, when circled, no major gaps were left between the wagons. With ox trains it was a different matter. Overnight camps were arranged in the rough outline of a fat arrow point with the wagons about the perimeter. A major gap was left at the base of the arrowlike area, through which the oxen could be driven in case of danger. Most of the time the oxen were permitted to graze on the prairie outside the camp protected by only one or two riders.

Blinded by the sun in their eyes, the defenders did not see the Cheyenne until they were upon them. The assault was incredibly swift and overpowering. The main body of the Cheyenne forced the breech between the wagons and was upon many of the crew before they could arm themselves. Some were preparing a simple meal of fatback, gravy, and sourdough hoecake. Others were laying out yokes and trace chains to harness the oxen. As a result most of the men were away from their rifles. They were forced to defend themselves as best they could with any weapon at hand.

When the attack came, Beck was at the point that received the major brunt of the attack. Shannon, however, was across the camp overseeing the roundup of the grazing oxen.

Shannon's horse was shot from under him. As it faltered, Shannon slid from the saddle jerking his rifle, saddlebags, and canteen free. His mount fell only a few feet from a buffalo wallow. Bullets dusted his heels as he dove into the depression.

This is it, Shannon thought to himself. *It would end here on a lonely prairie. Here he would die. But he would stand tall and take as many of the enemy with him as possible.*

Seeing Shannon down, a handful of braves stayed behind to deal with him. The rest joined the main attack on the wagons. He could hear sounds of battle from the train but dared not rise high enough to see what was occurring. As the firing slacked and the last cries of the wounded reached his ears, he realized the train was doomed and Beck with it. Beck, who over the past two years, had become a second father to Shannon.

Quickly checking his own situation, Shannon found he had only the shells in his belt loops and fifty rounds in his saddlebag. There was a small packet of pemmican, which he liked better than jerky, due to its sweetness from berries worked into the meat. There was precious little water, maybe half a canteen. Shannon knew the Cheyenne would wait him out, for without water he was at their mercy.

From the corner of his eye Shannon caught a slight movement in the tall grass. It was gently moving back and forth. Shannon smiled. He and Amble had tried that ruse on each other. Only, they tied string to a bush and caused it to move ever so slightly. This was an old trick to divert one's attention away from the real direction of an attack.

Shannon inched his way around facing the opposite direction. Using his boot knife he hastily dug out a shallow trench on the lip of the wallow through which he could see without exposing himself. Within moments there was a movement in the tall grass. Two warriors sprung to their feet to leap on Shannon. His rifle bucked twice and sprawled only a few feet in front of him were two dead braves. The first had been punched back by the powerful blow of the .44 in his chest and the other in death throes from a wound spurting blood from his throat. Shannon's bullet had glanced off the receiver of the brave's rifle severing fingers and ricocheting to slice open the neck. Shannon felt bile rising to his mouth. The two had been about his age and had acquitted themselves as true warriors.

Must it always be this way, thought Shannon, *kill or be killed? How long would it take to somehow develop an honorable peace between the white man and the red man? The Cheyenne were only defending their homes, families, lands, and way of life.*

Talk of the massacre of Black Kettle's people by Chivington, back in 1864, had made its rounds to every town, crossroads, and mining camp of the west. Chivington should have been executed for his crime and his men imprisoned. Instead they went free, while the Cheyenne mourned their dead and nourished their hatred for a bloodthirsty enemy without honor.

Chivington and his Third Colorado Volunteers had attacked the sleeping Cheyenne camp at dawn. Over two hundred had died in the massacre, many of them women and children. The conduct of Chivington and his men was inexcusable. Many of the dead were scalped and sexually mutilated. Black Kettle survived as chief of the Cheyenne, still believing that peace with honor could exist between the white man and the red man. Four years later in 1868 the Seventh Cavalry commanded by George Armstrong Custer smashed the peaceful village of Black Kettle, well within the Cheyenne reservation, nearly annihilating the occupants, killing Black Kettle and his wife, even scalping the Cheyenne Chief who championed peaceful coexistence.

Shannon thought of his hatred of those who had murdered his family and accepted the fact that the Cheyenne were no different. Yet if he had not killed, if he had tried to beg for mercy, shown weakness of heart and spirit, demonstrated the slightest shred of cowardice, the braves would have held him in contempt. There was honor in doing battle with a strong and fierce opponent. To die a warrior's death in battle with a strong enemy was an esteemed thing among the Cheyenne. They had died with honor, as Shannon hoped he would die.

By midafternoon the scorching sun had turned the buffalo wallow into a little corner of hell. Shannon's thirst was ever increasing. His mind began to wander as salty sweat crusted his shirt. Shannon knew that another day would present him with agonizing thirst and no way to assuage it. He thought of the bold streams of his childhood—the cold icy waters, which cascaded from the high tops, so cold that when you drank, you could feel it moving downward to the very pit of your stomach.

Shannon was roused from his reverie when a lark suddenly flared from the grass, sailed a ways, and fluttered back to earth. He eared back the hammer of his rifle. Now fully alert, so he thought, Shannon played the waiting game. A brave reared from his grassy cover but dropped back to the ground instantly. Shannon fired and missed, realizing his reflexes were not as quick as he thought. The heat, lack of water, and loss of sleep was slowing him down. Another warrior popped up. Again Shannon got off a shot but missed again; another wasted round. It finally got through to his muddled brain that he was being tricked into expending his precious hoard of ammunition.

As the day cooled toward evening, Shannon decided to try a ruse of his own. He had not fired a single round with his six-gun and doubted the Cheyenne knew he had one. Emptying the magazine of his carbine, he returned one round to the chamber. Taking his pistol from its holster he placed it close at hand and waited. After what seemed an eternity two warriors exploded from the grass, one to the left one to the right. He fired and then levered the rifle three times as they disappeared into the tall grass. The slamming of the receiver and the dull metallic click of the hammer on an empty chamber sent its own message. Their prey was out of ammunition. The brave closest to the wallow leapt up, sprinting toward Shannon. Shannon's forty-four spouted flames, clearly seen in the waning light, and the brave crumpled. Shannon watched the grass move as the other brave slipped away.

The third day brought its own particular brand of torture. There was no sweating. Loss of body moisture was all too evident. Lips were parched and cracked. Eyes were weak and hazy. A curious and deadly lethargy set in. His body refused to do whatever it was commanded. The sun, directly overhead, bored into the center of his brain. Some sixth sense told Shannon this was it. They would attack. He would be killed.

The last few drops of water were drained from the canteen. Within him there rose a battle lust, overpowering and deadly. He gripped the Colt in his right hand and his boot knife in the left. The long barreled Henry would be useless at such close quarters. Through parched bleeding lips, with croaking voice, he cursed the Cheyenne. He taunted them with insults and then they were on him. Before he could parry with the needle sharp point of the Arkansas toothpick or fire a shot, the smashing blow of a tomahawk turned the world black.

He awoke in a Cheyenne camp, hands bound, and a well-greased leather choke strap about his neck. He had been tethered like a horse to a stake. As full consciousness returned he could not fathom why his captors had let him live. More amazing was the fact they had obviously cared for his wounds and given him water and food. Yet none of that could he remember. Pangs of hunger and the burning thirst were gone.

With a practiced eye, as Beck had taught him, Shannon surveyed the entire village, pouring over every detail. From the number of tepees, women, children, and older men present he figured the village to have at least two hundred fifty to three hundred people. It was obvious the able-bodied were either on hunting parties or raids, since few young braves were in sight. He did not realize it, but this was the last moment of peace he would experience for months to come.

He had been spared to become a slave of the chief's sister. Not only was he at her mercy but that of the other women of the village. Daily Shannon was harnessed to a sled heavily loaded with firewood and buffalo chips. As he dragged the sled over dry gullies, through creek bottoms and grass-covered prairie the women constantly whipped him. The slender green river canes wielded by the women left weeping, infected welts on his back and chest. Ceaseless, demeaning ridicule filled him with an inner rage.

At first he answered his tormentors with English and Cherokee curses along with a few highly insulting phrases in Cheyenne, which he had quickly picked up from the women. Shannon shortly learned, however, not to make any threatening moves. When he did, the choke line was snapped taut, and he would be brought to his knees, gasping for breath.

His chief persecutor was inappropriately named Snow Flake. Shannon considered her to be an evil, vindictive hag. Only after he learned of the state to which she had been reduced did he actually begin to pity her. One son and her husband had been killed in the Chivington raid. The other son was crippled from a shot that shattered his hip. He was barely able to provide for himself and his mother. All of Snow Flake's pent-up anger was visited on Shannon. He had become the living sacrifice for her family members lost to the white man.

Unknown to the Cheyenne, Shannon had the legitimate right to plead a case for his release. If he could get the tribal council to hear his story, he felt certain he would not only be set free from servitude but perhaps elevated to a position of high esteem among the members of the tribe. None of the village spoke English. He would have to endure his abuse until an interpreter came to the camp, which was an impossible dream, or until he learned enough Cheyenne to plead his own case. The latter was his only hope.

The challenge was before him. He embraced it with relish. It would provide a way to occupy his mind during the endless days of toil. Different languages came to Shannon with relative ease. He was fluent in Cherokee. He had also picked up quite a bit of German from Stellwagen, as well as French from Rom, during the keelboat days. His growing ability to communicate with the Cheyenne brought some early relief. The choke strap was removed, and he was given greater freedom. Yet it was always under the watchful eye of Snow Flake or the other women of the village. Skills learned from the Cherokee were utilized, and slowly he began a claim to token acceptance among the braves.

Several months later he was confident of his ability to handle a defense before a tribal council. He only needed to determine a course of action that would precipitate a council.

Shannon had heard the women talking of the importance of the white slave to Snow Flake, especially how he had eased her burden and that of her crippled son in providing the daily necessities of life. It was also a fact that Snow Flake often permitted the other women to use Shannon for heavy chores. She was paid for the slave's labors with food and hides. Shannon felt confident if his life were threatened Snow Flake would do everything possible to have him spared. There was one sure way to force a crisis, which would draw the attention of the tribal council. He would attempt an escape.

The opportunity came sooner than expected. He was taken by the women to gather berries and nuts on a ridge and along the banks of a nearby stream. When the women bent to their tasks, Shannon slipped into the thickets and made a break for the river. Just as he reached the water two braves appeared on the opposite bank. They wheeled their ponies, boxed Shannon in, and herded him back to the camp. There they secured him once again to the rack reserved for captured foes.

About Shannon the council gathered. Snow Flake herself was beside her brother, pleading with him to spare the slave, saying, "He is mine. You gave him to me, my brother. My husband is dead. My son is dead. My living son is crippled. Without him we will starve. Who will feed my fires? Who will be my gatherer? Who will work for pelts and hides? Who will scrape and work the hides for clothing? Spare him my brother."

On and on she went with her wailing lament, groveling before the chief. Night Wolf, disgusted with her ceaseless whining, finally answered, "Leave me in peace woman! This night a council will gather, and his fate will be decided. Go to your lodge. Speak no more of the matter."

Shannon was freed of his bonds and stood before the council. His voice was hoarse due to the months of wearing the choke strap and its harsh frequent use. Yet with a strong voice he opened his defense addressing them in Cheyenne. His command of the language shocked them into silence and a flash of genuine dismay creased their faces.

He began, "Wise men of the Cheyenne, you have disgraced the honor of your nation and brought shame upon your clan."

Such words brought a chorus of angry retorts. As their words rose to a fever pitch due to Shannon's biting criticism, a brave burst through the circle, knife in hand. He was stopped short by the staff of a wizened medicine man, whose eyes were riveted upon Shannon and whose face was twisted with awesome fear.

"Let him speak what he will. Before my eyes flashed the vision of the white buffalo leaving our village. His head is low. He stumbles as he walks. He rumbles deep in his chest. Tears fall from his eyes. He weeps for the Cheyenne," the medicine man uttered.

Such sacred words from the shaman fell with the voice of death upon the Cheyenne. A murmur, akin to a death chant, went up from the entire village. Then came an eerie silence.

Shannon continued, "The spirits of my ancestors and yours are sad this day. They weep for the lost honor of the Cheyenne. They weep for bonds of trust broken. They weep for the betrayal and defiling of sacred oaths. They weep for your forgetfulness of solemn words of the past. They weep because you are filled with such great hatred for one white man you make them all your enemies." Shannon paused for a moment before continuing.

"I am Shannon Murphy, son of Shaun Murphy, grandson of Irish Murphy and his wife, Little Fawn, daughter of Yellow Sky, a chief of the Cheyenne. It was my grandfather who found the white buffalo wandering on the prairie. It was he who brought the bull calf to your camp. To you he was the most powerful of all totems. The white buffalo brought great fame and good fortune to you. Its spirit watched over you. Should he not now leave you; no longer bless you? You have treated harshly the descendant of the giver of the gift.

"In my body flows Cheyenne blood. I would cut my wrist and let it flow from me. It is tainted blood. You have treated me as an animal. You have tried to turn a warrior into a woman. You have shamed me, one who has counted coup many times. You have broken your word of friendship. The brotherhood given to my grandfather and his descendants is destroyed.

"I thought the word of the Cheyenne, once spoken, could never be retracted. That the word of this nation was inviolate. That the words wandered unseen in the sky above an everlasting testimony and witness. They live forever to always testify before you and the spirits of your ancestors. These witnesses gather about you this day and condemn you for what you have done. When word of this reaches the plains, the proud Cheyenne will be held in contempt by friends and enemies alike. I have spoken. Do what you will, but know I have spoken truth."

The shaman's reply was grave and commanding. "The wrong must be righted. The Great Spirit and the spirit of our ancestors are greatly disturbed. They look to us to restore their peace. We have but one excuse, none knew this man was of the family of Irish Murphy. Snow Flake in her bitterness and grasping has brought this upon us. The slave must be set free. She must be punished."

Shannon well knew it was a crucial moment for him and the Cheyenne. The pride and dignity of this clan within the Cheyenne nation had to be restored and made intact. What any one clan within the nation did reflected on the entire nation. He could at that very moment mount the nearest Indian pony and simply ride away a free man. He knew, however, that the valley of his dreams was located somewhere in the territory of the Southern and Northern Cheyenne or that of their allies. He needed their goodwill. It was imperative that he barter for the privilege of freely living among them.

During the early days of his captivity, Shannon had maintained his sanity by mentally building and rebuilding his dreams for the future. He was, in a sense, fleshing out the future if one was in the offing. It was no longer a simple homestead he envisioned building, rather a working ranch with a moderate cattle, but extensive horse herd. His eyes had never beheld such magnificent horses as the Cheyenne war ponies. The innate skill of the braves in breaking, riding, and caring for their mounts was incredible. Yet more incredible were the ponies themselves. They had more bottom than any horses Shannon had ever seen, especially for their size.

During his brief stay in New Orleans Shannon had once visited the race track. There he saw thoroughbreds race, breeds from Virginia and Kentucky, as well as the finest strains of riding and carriage horses, many standing sixteen hands. To mix the best of those bloodlines with the wild mustang, the Cheyenne war pony, would produce a horse to command premium prices. Shannon had seen enough and heard enough to know that the horse had as much to do with the winning and the settling of the West as the gun. For the first time Shannon envisioned combining a cattle and horse operation.

Again Shannon took a calculated risk. As the chief rose to speak he dared interrupt him. "I shall hold no grudge against my Cheyenne family. No hatred fills my heart. I have suffered. I have learned. I know the way of the Cheyenne, that of my grandmother. Your language is now mine. Your food nourished my body. Labors of slavery have made me strong. That which is bad can be turned into good. I ask a favor of the Cheyenne. Let me freely search for a far valley where I might live and grow strong sons. Let there be peace between our two families, the white and the red. When the winters are cold, and the tepees of my brothers are without meat you will come to my ranch and beef shall be yours for the mouths of your children and old ones."

A chorus of approval rose from the warriors and clan elders. The pipe was passed and the vows of brotherhood were again spoken.

Early the next morning Shannon rode from the camp astride one of the finest mountain-bred ponies he had ever seen. Trailing behind was a packhorse loaded with every kind of important truck. The outfit was gift enough, but the chief placed in Shannon's hands an incomparable offering, his own virtually new Henry rifle, army colt, bowie, and tinker knives. Shannon set his face to the high country and the search for his dreamed-of valley.

CHAPTER 4

Logan's Valley

Bright, warm, lazy days of summer had twice drifted past as Shannon moved about the high lonesome country. The rugged vastness, a seclusion of his own choosing, forced him inward, causing him to plumb the depths of his physical and mental resources. Many a man had been broken by such isolation and solitude. There were stories told about cook fires at night of those who wandered out of the wilderness with shuffling gait, glazed eyes, and babbling tongue—creatures more to be pitied than censured. Other accounts made the rounds. There were tales of partners who had cabin fever during long snowed-in winters resulting in murder and even cannibalism.

From time to time when the spring thaw came, a solitary traveler would chance upon a cabin and inside find the remains of a body. One suicide note read, "No longer can I live in this frozen hell. I go to a much warmer one." It was no illusion, no fabrication of a runaway imagination; mountain men lived a life on the edge. Often it was a delicate balancing act between sanity and insanity, between life and death, at the hands of those whose hunting grounds they had invaded; or a whimsical Mother Nature who was bane or blessing angel or demon.

From the Yellowstone to the Missouri, North Platte to the Snake, through territories of the Crow, Cheyenne, Sioux, Kiowa, Comanche, and Arapaho, Shannon moved as a ship without a rudder driven by whatever direction the wind of whim blew. Living off the land was not always easy, yet it was possible and at times nature's offerings allowed sumptuous fare.

His Cherokee name "Ghost Who Walks in Moccasins" was restored and soon well-known among the plains tribes. Into many a village he rode, without fear, to trade and more importantly to have contact with other humans.

Already the pinnacles were covered with snow and the high passes filled with mounting drifts. Mornings were becoming more and more frigid. Leaping from blankets to stir up the fire before pulling on pants and stomping into boots was becoming more and more distasteful to Shannon. He was too far back and too high up in the wild country. Lollygagging time was over. A retreat in which to ride out the fast approaching winter was now a necessity. If he didn't find one, there would be some mighty cold dawns.

Shannon quickly broke camp and was soon in the saddle, headed for what appeared to be a gap about three miles off. When he looked at the eastern sky, he knew trouble was headed his way. The warning in the good book must have been written about a sunrise such as he was seeing. Across the eastern horizon the sky had turned a glowing red to deep pink. The sun's light struggled to penetrate the growing gloom but was defeated by a steel gray sky, with rippling waves of clouds looking like the corrugated surface of a washboard. The breeze freshened with glacial cold.

Both the pony and Shannon were in for it, and the horse seemed to understand the situation far better than Shannon. When Shannon pointed his head toward that gap, he stepped out right smart. He must have shared Shannon's hope that it would be a pass leading down from the heights to some sheltered valley below.

To reach the gap was a steady climb upward. The higher they climbed the deeper the snow. At the mouth of the gap Shannon sat his horse dumbfounded. About a thousand feet below was a high mountain valley. That gap didn't lead out of it, it led into it. It was covered with snow that had fallen within the last three to four days. A stream, once boisterous and strong, moved sluggishly through the frozen landscape. In the frigid silence there came a quavering moan rising in intensity with volume subsiding into a tremulous shudder. The mustang's ears peaked up, his body became rigid and trembled. He pawed and stomped with one hoof, showing his reaction to the sound. As for Shannon, the hair on the back of his neck prickled and a wave of coldness coursed through his body from head to toe. No animal he knew made such a sound. If there were things as ghosts, haints, goblins, or spirits, and if they could speak, that had to be how they sounded. Just in case it was flesh and blood, Shannon eased his rifle from its scabbard. The pony was more than reluctant when urged through the gap into the valley below.

For a brief while the only sound was that of dry powdery snow crunching under hoofs and the howl of a growing wind dancing and swirling across the valley floor as it lifted wisps of dry snow into the air. Rounding the last switchback leading to the valley floor, again the moan was heard. This time

Shannon almost jumped from his horse, for the sound seemed to come from underfoot. In front of him, not more than ten feet away was a man covered with snow. In fact, he probably would have ridden right over him if his head had not moved.

Swiftly brushing away the snow there was revealed a giant of a man, more dead than alive. Only when Shannon had stripped the snow from his legs was the ugly truth revealed. His leg was in the jaws of a grizzly bear trap. How long he had lain there Shannon did not know. It was imperative, if the two and the animals were to live, that shelter be found, and that right quick. Night was coming on and with dawn a fresh blizzard.

At first there was no response from the injured man. "Old man, can you hear me? Answer if'n you can," Shannon said as he began chaffing the injured man's hands between his, then he massaged his arms, neck, and face with little observable result. Rummaging in his trampaddak Shannon took out a fire starter. A crushed bird's nest torn in half and mixed with finely rubbed fir bark was the best starter known to man. From a nearby deadfall, twigs and small branches were gathered. Steel was put to flint and in a brief time a small fire was going. A coffeepot was quickly filled with snow and soon coffee was in offing. Coffee should be strong enough to float a horseshoe but the circumstances called for stronger. When the grounds settled, it would float a horseshoe on the horse! Touching the almost frozen lips of the hapless man with the scorching brew had its effect. He gulped the liquid fire like a dog lapping water. The first word he spoke was "More." After the third cup he sort of reared up on his side, lifted his arm pointing a finger and said, "There, over there!" then slumped back.

He was pointing to a bluff across the creek some several hundred yards away. About thirty feet up the slope there appeared to be a ledge screened by a thick wall of fir trees. With greater effort he rose again on one elbow and pointed to the same place. This time the words were filled with urgency as he grunted, "There, damn you! There! There!" That time he really got Shannon's attention.

The only thing more surefooted than a mountain-bred mustang is a mountain goat or a long-legged mule. Shannon didn't have either of the last two, but he sure had one savvy pony. With steps as dainty as a schoolmarm walking the aisle on her wedding day, he eased across the icy bottom and the frozen banks of the creek. Behind the screen of trees there was a bench clear of ice with only a powdering of fine snow which had filtered though the trees.

What greeted Shannon's eyes was a sight to behold. Invisible from below, due to the screen of trees, was a huge overhanging rock ledge creating a rock shelter the size of a small ranch house. Since time before telling, those who had occupied it, for either short or long stays, had carefully fitted a rock wall some forty feet long from floor to ceiling. The rock above had been smoked black from the fires of ages past. What a story it could tell if it could speak.

Shannon had heard of another such place. A tinker traveling through the mountains once spent the night in the Murphy's cabin. He told of a time when he had waited out a harsh winter's ice storm on the upper Cape Fear River at a place called Raven Rock. He described the cliff that had been undercut by the raging spring floods of the river creating a tremendous rock shelter that by that time was well above the highest flood stages of the water. Like this shelter it must have been a refuge for the wandering hunter, trapper, or what have you since remotest times.

Whoever it was below had occupied the shelter. There was an ample supply of wood so Shannon started a fire. The man was badly hurt and possibly dying. Stepping out on the bench, he cut two stout poles and prepared to walk down the slope to the bottom below. Already he had stripped his horse and pack animal. When he rubbed them down with a few handfuls of dry grass plucked from the sheltered side of the trail, they seemed grateful. Had Shannon known what the return trip would ultimately cost him, he might not have gone. Yet to do otherwise was unthinkable.

Shannon looked into pain-glazed eyes as he stooped to a dangerous task. He could with brute strength force open the jaws of the trap. Townsfolk wouldn't think it possible. They would use a weight or a prize pole to help. More often than not when a bear trap was set, it was a one-man job. The hapless victim had probably let the jaws slip while setting the trap and had trapped himself. But, to open the trap would require the use of both of his hands calling upon every ounce of strength in his arms and shoulders. While he held the trap open, the injured leg had to be lifted from its jaws. He couldn't do both without the danger of injury to himself and additional suffering for the trapped man.

"Old man, are you listening? Open those eyes. Listen up! You've got to lift that leg, pulling your foot from the trap when I open 'er up," Shannon said. There was no response. Shannon hated to do it, but he slapped him hard a couple of times. His eyes flew open and he gave Shannon a graveyard look. It would have withered a live oak tree.

"Listen to me. Now that I have your attention, do what I tell you. I'm going to open that trap and you pull your leg out," Shannon repeated.

"Open 'e-r up and by damn I'll get the foot out. Then I'm gonna' slap you from here to the Mormon settlements," the man replied.

What neither realized was that as soon as those frozen steel jaws released the leg every nerve at the injury site would start coming alive and the leg would ultimately explode with pain. Shannon grabbed the jaws and began to slowly force them open. The man's scream almost made him lose his grip. "My God, he's fainted!" said Shannon. "What am I going to do?" Powerful shoulders, hugely muscled chest as well as strong wrists and hands could only hold the trap open so long. There was only one thing to do, since the trap chain was not anchored. He now had to jerk the open trap from the clutches of a frozen earth, and with one tremendous heave cast it aside while escaping the lightning fast snap of the jaws. He made it, but barely.

The trap's deadly mission was plainly revealed. It had nearly amputated the foot well above the ankle. Merciful unconsciousness allowed Shannon to slit the trouser leg. Proud flesh, bone fragments, massively bloated calf, and streaks of red running to the groin told him gangrene had set in and that death was only playing a brief waiting game.

Slipping from his heavy coat, Shannon hurriedly made a crude travois by buttoning the coat and running one of the poles up either side and out the sleeves. Placing it beside the trapper Shannon rolled him on it and finally succeeded in pulling the virtually lifeless form on to the rock ledge and into the shelter.

Shaving thin slices of jerky into a pot with melted snow and a few dried herbs Shannon created a hot and not too unhearty broth. After downing two cups of the steaming mixture the man spoke. "Name is Logan," he said before drifting again into the oblivion of unconsciousness. Logan needed rest, that was for sure, but it was imperative that Shannon tried to do what he could about the leg. It seemed hopeless but a body had to try.

"Logan, it's time to work on that leg. Understand me, there is not much I can do. I could try to amputate," Shannon said. With that, Logan let out a howl. "No mother's son is going to take my foot off. I ain't no animal to be cut on, chopped at, or snubbed up."

In some fashion Shannon had to get him to understand that he would not attempt to take the foot off. If he did, it would do no good. Logan was going to die, but Shannon didn't want to hit him over the head with it. He handed Logan a little cloth bag about the size of a large walnut. It was packed with anise seeds, which, when chewed had a narcotic effect. It was a trick Stellwagen had learned on one of his army tours and shared with Shannon during the keelboat days. Since that time he had always carried one or two in his possibles bag.

"Logan, chew on this slowly. It'll help the pain, and God knows you will need it," Shannon said.

"Go to hell, boy, I ain't no lap baby to chaw on no sugar tit," Logan replied.

Shannon reached down and lightly pressed the bloated flesh at the site of the wound. Logan growled through clenched teeth, "Tarnation, watch what you're doing. If I could get up from here, I'd show you what real pain is. I'd retch down your throat and pull you wrong side out."

"If you think what I just did hurt, well, cheer up for the worst is yet to come. When I start cleaning up that leg, you'll plead for anything to stop the pain. Now start chewing, 'cause I'm starting on that wound," Shannon replied.

It's hard to understand why people get so darned ungrateful when another tries to help them. Shannon recalled an instance years before back home when one of the Younce boys got his leg caught in a deadfall. He was bellowing like a bull that had been balled when Shannon got to him and immediately he started telling him what to do and how to do it, but mostly why in all that was holy hadn't he got there sooner! Shannon toted the ungrateful cuss near a mile to his pap's cabin. When he put him down on the porch, he commenced telling the whole clan how clumsy Shannon was, and how he had jostled him coming up the mountain. He really put on a shine when he told them Shannon had nearly dropped him just because a little old timber rattler coiled by the path had started singing his song. Shannon felt he would have been a heap better off if he had thrown him down by the path and picked up the rattler.

Logan had relented. He was working the wad of anise seeds like a chaw of good tobacco. In a short while he dropped off to sleep, but from time to time winced with pain. Working as swiftly as possible with a solution of herbs and warm water, the frozen, putrid flesh began to slough off revealing just how badly the leg was injured. Shattered bone fragments protruded and the smell, since the flesh had thawed, was awful. God, what a predicament!

How helpless one feels in the face of such unforeseen circumstances. This was and wasn't new to Shannon. There had been more than a few misadventures to deal with in his young life. He'd been mauled by a black bear when he got between her and her cubs. He'd slipped on the damp mossy face of a rock cliff and tumbled catawampus about thirty feet, skinning everything on the outside and bruising most of what was on the inside.

Before his pa went off to war he made Shannon face up to some of the harsh realities of life. His pet raccoon, as mischievous a little devil as one had ever seen, was bitten by a rabid fox. His pa killed the fox and buried it deep. Shannon put his coon in a pen and several days later it was evident that he too was rabid. His pa sat him down for a man-to-man talk.

"Son, that coon of yours is suffering something awful. He's a goner for sure. You have a man-size decision to make. Kill that coon or sit by and watch him die the worst of all deaths," his pa said.

"But, Pa, can't you do it? I mean kill him like you did the fox. Don't know as how I can," Shannon replied.

"Son, you have to take the responsibility. That coon is yours. It's your call. Have you forgotten what I have tried to teach you since you were no bigger than a tadpole? If you are going to be a man, then do what a man must do," his pa said.

It took Shannon a minute to think over what his pa had said. "Pa, remember Old Man Nations? He took awful sick, having them fits and all. Then he laid on that corn shuck mattress for weeks doubled up with pain. Everybody said he was going to die, and he wouldn't let nobody help him. Why he cussed and yelled and threw things at anybody that tried. Nobody just up and put him out of his misery," Shannon replied.

His ma cleared her throat and spoke his nickname, rarely used except in those soft moments of tenderness. "Cricket, Old Man Nations never asked anybody to help him in or out of his miseries. That coon is a different case. I'll bet if that coon could talk, he would ask you to help him," his mother explained. Shannon picked up his rifle and went out to do what he had to do.

If Shannon tried to take the foot off with nothing but axe and knife, Logan would surely bleed to death. He had no pitch to coat the stump and little in the way of needle and thread for sewing. The stump might be cauterized with hot iron or gunpowder, but that was at the best tricky. Everything he did would only increase Logan's pain. Gangrene had completely invaded his thigh and the mounting fever brought a blessed torpor. Shannon decided to do nothing to increase Logan's pitiable state. He would stay with him, keeping him as comfortable as possible, and in the end give Logan a decent burial. This meant he was trapped in the high valley until the spring thaw. That was not the most delightful of prospects.

How Logan lived as long as he did, Shannon did not know. He must have been superhuman. For endless winter-bound days Logan eased in and out of a state of semiconsciousness. During the lucid times Shannon talked him to death. Whether he heard it or not, Shannon poured out all of the hurt, pain, suffering, and disappointment of his life. There were times when Logan would nod or grunt in approval or disapproval with what was said. Only on one occasion did he seem to light up with the fires of understanding. It was when Shannon spoke of his search for a ranch site in the land of the Cheyenne and of his days among them as a slave before gaining release.

For a week Logan grew visibly worse, scarcely breathing. At times a soft groan would escape his lips, or there would be a sudden intake of breath as jagged flashes of pain racked his body.

Then one day he was as bright as a new twenty-dollar gold piece and as talkative as a magpie.

"Ain't got no kith or kin. You've stuck by me, boy, and give as much comfort as you could to ease my dying. Never did take to the notion of dying alone. Hate to go without words being said over me," Logan said.

"Don't fret none, Logan. We've come this far together and I give you my solemn word I'll tend to things," Shannon replied.

With a voice much weaker, Logan spoke to Shannon like his pa did that last night in the burning cabin. "Shannon, over the past years I picked right many pockets of gold from these high mountain streams. Once found a glory hole of jewelry rock. You could crumble the quartz with your fingers and pick out the gold. Now it's yours, boy. Old Logan's farewell gift. It's hid in a hole above the ledge just over my head. Hit, the furs and the animals are yours. You said you dreamed of your own ranch some day. Well, what's there ought to get you started right smart," Logan revealed.

With that he heaved a sigh and the stillness of death slowly crept over him. Shannon reached over, closed Logan's eyes, and wept.

How strange the closeness brought on by adversity and need. No one had ever needed Shannon before, and he suddenly realized how important it was to a human being to be needed. Shannon's mind turned to his aunt Sadie, who lived two hollows over from his family's cabin in the Smokies. She was a tiny lady, bent over with the weight of years. She would say with the deepest pathos in her voice how useless she felt since Uncle Shad had died and the boys gone off to war.

All during the remaining days of that winter Shannon not only mourned the loss of Logan but found himself incredibly frustrated having no one to care for. He lavished attention on the animals. They, in a way, became his salvation.

One day Shannon fell down in fits of laughter when he realized he had been carrying on a serious conversation with a pack mule and expected an answer. He realized quickly that his sanity was more to be questioned than that of the mule.

A few weeks later Shannon awakened to the steady trickle of water falling from the icicle-covered ledge on the shelter. Spring's thaw was on the way. Shannon made preparations to leave what he would forever call Logan's Valley. The first day the pass was open he left the valley behind and headed for the nearest settlement, following Logan's directions.

CHAPTER 5

Frontier Justice

Like some specter out of the bowels of Hades, Shannon rode into the town of Slocom. Logan, before his death, had plainly described the trail out of the valley in terms of landmarks along the way. From the lightning-seared blue spruce, due south to the cliff marked with a white quartz streak like a sprung S, Shannon was to follow the faint animal trail from the base of the marked cliff up and over the top to a valley far below. The creek along the valley floor was to be followed downstream to its junction with a larger stream that was to be followed for several days before reaching Slocom.

He had asked Logan how the place had been named Slocom, and Logan spun an amazing yarn as to its origins. It had been for years a mining camp with no big strikes, but decent pay for a hard week's work with pan or sluice box, shovel or sledge if needed. Small pockets of color abounded in the area, but no one seemed to find the mother lode. The camp was soon transformed into a respectable and quite stable small town. Merchants, miners, and saloonkeepers moved in, along with a stable and smithy. There was a preacher, a schoolteacher, and a doctor of sorts. Whenever they gathered at one of the saloons and the talk turned to gold, the consensus of opinion was dust and nuggets were slow to come by. "Slow to come by" was shortened to Slocom, and the town was officially named.

Logan's buckskins were in shambles. They were ripped and patched, darkened with sweat and the smoke of campfires. Leggin moccasins were worn to shreds. An unruly mass of curly thick black hair hung well down on his shoulders and blended with the brush pile on his face. All who looked halfway close wondered if his six-foot-four body was outside trying to get into his buckskins, or inside trying to get out. No doubt about it, Shannon was the perfect picture of the hind end of bad times.

Every day of the six-week ride to Slocom, Shannon traveled in a state of acute alertness, while at the same time his mind churned over and over the prospects of the days ahead. Logan's legacy would open a new world for him. He had no idea what his former investments with Adler and Co. might be worth currently, if anything. Nonetheless he had a start, if he could keep it. Now was the time to come to grips with himself and decide what he truly wanted out of life; not just what he could get but what he could give. His pa, Beck, and Logan had all taught him by their acts that getting and giving were the two inseparable sides of the single coin of life. Either without the other was no good.

Before Shannon was the threshold of a country, which was big, wild, and dangerous. Only the quick of mind, steady of hand, and bold of spirit would make even a small contribution to its future. Already he had seen the takers, the destroyers. Human parasites of every ilk were in plenteous supply. They cared not a whit for the rights, property, or lives of others. Either under the guise of respectability or open dishonesty they plotted to deprive others of their hard-earned rights and property.

Waldroop's discussions on the law during the river days were finally making sense to him, especially the arguments from English common law and the simple explanations he gave. His saying that the rights of Shannon's fist stopped where Waldroop's nose began now took on significant meaning; one person's rights stopped where another person's began. It made good sense but Shannon was still puzzled. "What is going to keep my fist from hitting your nose or you from trampling over my rights?" he asked Waldroop on one occasion.

"Son, officers of the law arrest you and the courts pass sentence. This protects you," Waldroop replied.

"But, Waldroop, on the frontier there is no law and there are no courts. Who protects your rights then?" Shannon asked.

"Then, Shannon, you must protect your own rights. Until the rule of law comes to new territories one must be strong enough and determined enough to secure what is theirs. Keep reading those Blackstone books and the Bible. They'll help you," Waldroop said.

"That sure is a heap to think about," Shannon replied.

"Shannon, boy, where there is no law ultimately each man stands alone to protect his own rights, and, if he is much of a man, the rights of others, especially those who cannot defend themselves. The mark of a genuine human being is not that he accomplishes what is right all the time, but he tries to do just that. This means you have to constantly struggle, deep in your soul, to determine the right and the wrong of things," Waldroop explained.

Shannon attracted an abundance of attention as he rode down the dusty street and tied up at the rail of the Wells Fargo office. The agent looked to be a crusty veteran of many a battle with man and nature. His face was leathery, crisscrossed with wrinkles. His short cropped sun-bleached hair somewhat reminded Shannon of one porcupine whose quills had been cropped. Penetrating blue eyes looked Shannon full in the face. One could tell he had been down the river and over the mountain.

His eyes fairly bulged when Shannon placed the sacks of dust and nuggets on the counter. Without a word he went about the business of an assay. With a stubby pencil he wrote an amount on a scrap of paper. This time Shannon's eyes bulged. In those deerskin pouches was a fortune.

"Mister, my name is Shannon, Shannon Murphy. Would you put all this on an account in my name with Wells Fargo? Seems most everywhere I go there's Wells Fargo," Shannon requested.

"Shannon, I'm George Ferguson. Let me fill out the papers for you and you can draw on your account at any of the Wells Fargo banks. In fact, right now, we have over five hundred offices from Missouri to California. But don't you want some walking around money?" Mr. Ferguson said.

"Outside there are four bails of prime pelts on the pack horses. That will more than do me for anything I might have a hankering for," Shannon replied.

After folding his letters of credit and putting them in his belt pouch, Shannon thanked Mr. Ferguson and headed for the door.

"Just a second, Shannon. You walk easy, sleep light, and watch your back trail. A wild bunch rode in last night; among them a couple of would-be bad men. Their kind will slit your throat for less than a dab of what you're carrying," Mr. Ferguson said.

"Mr. Ferguson, anyone, and I mean anyone, who thinks they can take what I have then let them have it. They had better make their peace with the man upstairs before they try. And, mister, that ain't no brag, just plain unvarnished truth. By the way, where can I find an honest fur buyer?" Shannon replied.

"You don't mince words, do you, Shannon? I'd take my furs to Wilson's Store. They don't come any better, and you can trade out for your needs," Mr. Ferguson said.

As Shannon's footsteps faded on the plank porch Ferguson thought to himself, *That is a young man to be reckoned with.* Ferguson had seen a few like him, self-contained, always in control, sure in a quiet way of who they were and where they were going. Behind his eyes there lingered a dangerous darkness, which hinted at a streak of sheer raw power—Shannon would be more than a handful in any kind of serious encounter.

The four bales of prime pelts brought a right handsome price. Wilson had seen few furs packed as those Shannon deposited on his counters. The pelts, weighing about one and one-half pounds each were squeezed into fifty-pound deerskin bales. Bales, such as these, were normally sold by trappers at the rendezvous at a price of three to six dollars a pelt. There were over three hundred prime pelts for which Shannon received almost sixteen hundred dollars. That was more than enough to outfit Shannon with supplies for a long search of the high lonesomes, and if it could be bought, to pay for land as well as cover any incidental expenses. He wanted to find that valley, file on it and, if necessary, locate a lawyer who would handle the matter of deeds.

Deeds were tricky instruments, and Shannon wanted no land unless he held the timber and mineral rights. Shannon had spent hours with Waldroop discussing the tricks of the trade when it came to executing deeds. He had learned of the different types of deeds and especially difficulties, which might be confronted by one holding a quitclaim deed. Shannon was fascinated by a deed as recorded in the book of Genesis, the first Old Testament book. When Abraham purchased a field from Ephron, the Hittite, the deed was drawn up to include a cave within the field and all of the trees in the field. Thus the field was sold along with the timber rights. When law came to the area, Shannon wanted to be certain that his claims to the land were well protected.

Yet Shannon was not convinced, to his own satisfaction, that he should immediately continue the search. The bitterly lonely ordeal after Logan's death and the refreshing of being in the company of others told him he had experienced enough remoteness, solitary days, and companionless nights for a while. Before he settled in to spend the future building a dream, he wanted to get a larger, a greater exposure to what was occurring in the westward movement.

Not one obstacle was in his way. He looked much older than his twenty years, but one grew up quickly or not at all in the West. He would not lose his dream, only delay its fulfillment. After all was said and done dreams were like fruit on a tree. Plucked green they were disappointing, bitter to the taste, and at times caused pain if eaten. If picked when mature, succulent, and ripe, the fruit was deeply satisfying.

He left most of his trampaddix at the Wells Fargo office for safekeeping. Taking only saddlebags, rifle, and newly bought clothes, Shannon headed for the hotel. If anybody had ever needed a bath, shave, and change of clothes, it was Shannon. Looking at himself in the mirror he was as much changed as he had been when he saw himself at the end of the Mississippi days. His figure reflected in the mirror was huge. Facing him was a man to be reckoned with.

His mind swiftly journeyed through the last four to five years of his life. The days of wrestling the sweeps on the barge, the endless hours of poling the keelboat against the current, periodic battles with the river rats, thieves of the highest order, the physical labors of the Cheyenne camp, and the regaining of his Cherokee name "Ghost Who Walks in Moccasins," the time in Logan's valley whose powder and shot provided daily work with rifle and pistol, deadly combats with Indians and half-breed trappers, hours of training by Rom with knife and in the art of foot and fist fighting, which the French called savate, all had gone into the making of the marked physical change. Butternut sailcloth britches covered the high-laced moccasins in which a razor-sharp bowie knife nestled, snugged against his leg. Between the shoulders of the buckskin shirt hung his tinker-made knife in its soft sheath, and slung over his hips was a gun belt with a brand-new Colt riding easy. The six-gun was bought at Wilson's, his first purchase.

Levi's pants were something else. They wore like iron. Wilson said a man named Levi in California started making the trousers out of sail canvas for the miners who were mighty hard on their clothes. They outlasted all other brands and had become the most sought-after type of pants for cowboys, miners, and farmers. They were a bit rough on first wearing but after several washings and pounding out on a rock none better or more comfortable could be found.

The rumble of Shannon's stomach brought an end to his musing. He left the hotel and stepped into the street. Before him was a pitiful scene. A half-drunk buffalo hunter was leading an apparently young Indian woman by a choke rope. Shannon felt his throat closing, remembering the Cheyenne slave days.

The woman turned and stumbled. When she did, Shannon saw the white film over her eyes and heard the mumbling of Sioux incantations. On her face was a strange, stunned expression—that of one emotionally blighted. She was a holy woman, blind, but with great powers among the Sioux. The furies rose within Shannon. The indignities already heaped upon her by her captors were only a prelude to those of the future. In the end her white captors would leave her ravaged, broken, and lifeless body somewhere out in the prairie. It could not be tolerated.

Shannon snatched the cord out of the man's hand and placed the woman behind him. She seemed to understand the words he spoke in Cheyenne. The "buffaler" wheeled with the speed of a good cutting horse, saying, "Who the hell do you think you are? I found that woman out on the prairie, and by gawd, she's mine. Take your hands offen' her or I'll hang your hide over a corral rail."

As he spoke, he turned toward Shannon. That face! It was one whose image was etched on his brain; drooping eye, the scar across eyebrow and forehead, and on the back of his hand the mark of Shannon's knife. By this time a crowd had gathered.

"I don't know your name, and if I did it wouldn't be worth spit. Maybe you remember me. Back when I was pure tee green you stole the gold my pa give me. Then you shot me and dumped me over a cliff to die. Well, I'm alive and all the green is wore off. I have but one word for you. I'm going to wreck your wagon, rip off your wheels, stick a clevis in your nose, and lead you to the waters of destruction," Shannon said.

"My name is Kinnard and if you think you can tear down my playhouse then walk right up to it and have a try," the man tauntingly replied.

Shannon did not realize how close the man was to him until his head was snapped back with a slap of Kinnard's open palm. That did it! Back in the hills no greater insult occurred than for someone to deliver such a blow. To be slapped in the face with a flat open palm always led to a no-holds-barred, knuckle-busting, tooth-jarring fight. The insult plus all of the pent-up anger over the treatment at the tavern on the way to Louisville erupted within Shannon. There was a split second of blind fury, then a cold deadly calm settled over him. Shannon was going to beat this hulk of a man into a bloody pulp.

Standing directly in front of Shannon, his opponent dropped his hands to his sides daring him to strike. The man was a fool, he expected Shannon to go for his jaw. Instead he ripped a right, pivoting, and throwing all of his weight behind the blow. Shannon's fist almost disappeared into Kinnard's lower belly. It was a low blow. He intended it to be. The soft underbelly, that's where they live. Although he bent double with a groan, his recovery was incredibly fast. He straightened and hit Shannon with a looping right. Shannon slipped part of the blow with his forearm, but enough of the fist, which seemed as big as a buffalo hump, landed on the side of Shannon's head. His vision was momentarily blurred by shooting stars racing across his brain.

Kinnard was not only big, but also strong, and had enough whiskey in him to be slightly immune to pain. Standing toe-to-toe they slugged it out.

Shannon's shirt was ripped, a lump was rising on his jaw and the corner of his mouth was split. His opponent's face was another picture. The stiff left jabs had opened cuts over both eyes. Blood trickled from his nose, the result of repeated blows. Whenever he dropped his guard, Shannon's right slashed through the opening with devastating effect. Both men were gasping for breath, but Shannon was quickly gaining his second wind. The fight was a long way from over, yet in that moment Shannon knew the victor would be him.

Unexpectedly, and with deceptive quickness, Kinnard clinched with Shannon. His arms encircled Shannon's waist. One fist was turned inward with the knuckles against Shannon's spine. He began to squeeze applying the full pressure of his arms and shoulders. In a crippling bear hug he lifted Shannon off the ground. A moment of panic hit Shannon, then was gone.

"Now," Shannon said to his opponent, "You'll learn some things about brawling that are new." Stretching out his arms with cupped hands inward he brought them with all of his strength in a ruinous blow over both ears at the same time. The sudden pressure trapping air in the ear canal, with no place to go, burst both eardrums. Kinnard's scream that ended in a whimper didn't sound human. The buffaler's arms dropped, and Shannon went to work in earnest.

Only Shannon's blows kept him upright against a hitching rail. As he slid to the ground, Shannon turned to walk away.

"Watch out!" yelled Ferguson, who had joined the crowd. Turning, Shannon saw the half-crazed lout drawing a bowie knife from his boot. His eyes were filled with a frenzied lust to kill.

The tinker knife, a slim razor-sharp piece of steel, leapt from its sheath behind Shannon's neck. For an instant sunlight danced along its deadly edge. It split the air, whispering its song of death, and buried itself in the man's neck. Rom had taught him well.

The dead man's two companions, recovering from the shock of what had happened, reached for their guns. It was their undoing.

When little bigger than a tick on a dog, Shannon was practicing with rifle and pistol. He didn't have any fancy handguns, only an old single shot North muzzleloader. His pa hadn't believed in sticking a gun in a waistband or stuffing it down the top of a boot. Shannon's pa believed in a holster worn on the hip handy to the shooting hand. So when it was drawn the pistol would come up in a vertical motion right to the target.

When facing man or beast, Shannon was told if he used the crossdraw or pulled his gun from his waistband, the muzzle would cross his target, making it harder to hit. The way his pa showed it to him was having him shoot at twigs on a tree limb. He found it ten times harder to clip a twig growing horizontally from a limb than one growing vertically. Shannon quickly learned to line his sights on the twig pointing straight up and pop it right off. His pa had kept telling him that lifting a gun straight up from the holster gave a lot more area to shoot at than he had if he swung the muzzle from side to side. For hours on end Shannon would hang that old horse pistol down by his side, up with it, and let fly. There was many a locust post back in the hills, which could testify that Shannon had been their way.

Shannon palmed the Colt and it slid from his holster in a blur of movement. His attention first centered on the man to his left. It was no time for niceties. He could have easily shot him in the shoulder, arm, or leg. At that distance Shannon could put three shots inside a half-dollar slip shooting, but there were two guns to deal with. The first man was hit just above the bridge of his nose. There was a tug at Shannon's shirt and a burning streak crossed his side. Already he was dropping into a well-practiced crouch with left leg stretched out and right knee on the ground.

A gun blasted a second time. In his haste, the last of the three missed. Shannon didn't. Twice Shannon's rounds made holes in his chest. Frothy blood appeared at the corner of his opponent's mouth. Shannon's second shot had been a bit low and probably drove a rib through the lungs. Without a sound, the man slid slowly down the porch post and rolled to his side. There is no quiet like that of a street or bar room when the gunfire stops. Momentarily everything comes to a screeching halt, as if to pay homage to those dead and injured. Not a single eye of accusation was turned upon Shannon. Spectators along the street saw that it was a fair fight and that he had only defended himself, perhaps too well!

Shannon walked over to Ferguson to thank him for the warning. "Ferguson, I'll always be in your debt for giving me that warning. I hate to ask, but there is a favor you can do for me and for your town. Will you get the Holy Woman back to her people?" Shannon said.

"Shannon, there's a half-breed working on a ranch about four or five miles out. I'll see that he returns her to her village. But more than that, I'll have him tell them what happened here," Mr. Ferguson replied.

At the breaking of dawn the next day, Shannon was on his way. A lot of water would have to pass under the bridge before he could begin to flesh out his dreams.

CHAPTER 6

Last Cattle Drive

Months had turned into years, three of them in fact, marching rank on rank, like an army passing in review. With them Shannon had changed. On the anvil of western life he had been pounded with the hammers of adversity and rivalry. The whole of his being had been abused like ore from a furnace until purged, all dross removed. Only steel, which had been abused by the pounding of the blacksmith's hammer, heated and reheated, quenched in baths of oil or water, shaped and formed in a tempering process, became strong enough to hold a keen cutting edge. After such years Shannon emerged from the smithy of frontier life ready to face any challenge, threat or circumstance. By his middle twenties Shannon was an individual forged into a maker of the West.

Thinking back over those days Shannon remembered some events with keen regrets, others with a joyous satisfaction. Saddle-weary days of trail herding gave him ample time to weigh the past and more firmly plan the future. He was more convinced than ever that ranching was the immediate goal of his life, and the sooner the better.

An Abilene trail drive had been his first as trail boss. Two thousand ornery longhorns to be driven from the Texas panhandle to Abilene were in his charge. In 1867 Abilene was next to nothing as a town. There were only log huts with soddy roofs and few people. Four years later, with a railhead established, it was one of the worst hell-raising cow towns ever birthed. It had all the cultural refinements eagerly sought after by cowboys, if you could call them that: gambling halls, saloons, a theater, and enough bawdy houses to accommodate a good part of the U.S. Western Army Command.

The drive had not been without its dangerous moments, the worst of which occurred after crossing into Kansas Territory. Rainfall had been scant and sufficient water was hard to find. Muddy Creek was, according to a lone rider's information, still running sluggishly.

Topping a rise above the creek were five hard-bitten riders. One glance announced them as jayhawkers, herd cutters—cutthroats that lived off herds moving across Kansas to the cattle towns. They were a sorry lot of malingerers, yet each was well mounted and armed. Shannon turned slightly sideways in the saddle and eased the thong from the hammer of his Colt as he rode toward the group.

Their leader spoke bluntly and to the point. "We're the Jessup brothers. We believe you've picked up some of our cows in passing though so we're cutting your herd. Figure a hundred and fifty head ought to be about right."

Shannon framed an unexpected reply. "Friend, haven't you ever read the Good Book where Moses when he was leaving Egypt said, 'Our cattle also go with us.' It says us, not you. Now you wouldn't want to go against the Book and call Moses a liar, would you?"

His very words indicated Shannon was on the prod. Something about the bunch had royally cranked up his disgust for all men who lived by taking that which they had never worked for, and for which other men had given their sweat and blood.

A devil-may-care lust for battle roared through Shannon. The two outside riders slowly moved their mounts in order to flank him. One of the Jessups looked over his shoulder then inched his horse forward and said, "If you don't like the idea of a hundred and fifty head, then we'll just take them all," and began easing his hand toward his gun butt.

It was no time for niceties. In an instant it would be do or die. Shannon's Colt, as if thinking his thoughts, seemed to mysteriously leap from holster to hand. The muzzle blossomed with a halo of death. Two shots, so close together they seemed as one, echoed through the afternoon quiet. A stillness, which was eternal, settled over both Jessup brothers. They tumbled from their saddles, quivered for a moment in spasms of death then lay unmoving. Disbelief masked the faces of the Jessup riders. They had seen fast guns before. Among the group there was not one man without an abundance of gun savvy. To the man, however, not one would ever dare try to match, much less think they could beat, Shannon's lighting draw. Cold chills moved up their spines. If anyone made a move the man before them with granite face and unblinking gaze would empty at least two more saddles.

Anger gave a sharp edge to Shannon's words. "There's three more in my gun," he said. "Unbuckle your gun belts and let them fall. If you want to make a play, do it. Four of my men are behind you holding Winchesters. Not one of them will interfere. It's you and me. They'd love to join the party but they know there will be nothing but three empty saddles left when they do. Now, get off those horses and shuck your guns!"

As they dismounted four of Shannon's crew rode up. "You mean there's none left for us?" Funk said with a smile on his face.

"Give their guns back and let me have at 'em."

"Now, Funk," Grat said, "don't try to hog it all. Why, I want in on this. Haven't shot a two-legged polecat in several months. Reckon these will stink as much as that last one? These sure do look ripe." One of the Hatton twins chimed in, "Not that I want to spoil your fun, but give this some serious thought. If you kill all of them, then we'll have to bury the whole lot. It's a hot day and I never did take to the shovel. If you are going to kill them, at least let one live so's he can bury the others. Then we'll kill him leaving us only one grave to dig." That started the herd cutters begging for mercy. Even when they were funning, Shannon's men could be mighty intimidating.

"Grat, you and Funk take their gun belts and hang them over their saddle horns. Empty guns and belt loops. Shuck the shells out of those Winchesters, and then have these fine gentlemen sit down and remove their boots. Take their horses, guns, and boots several miles due south and stake out the horses. A good long walk will give these misguided souls time to reflect upon their waywardness. Let me give you three a word of warning. If we ever lay eyes on you again, we'll hang every cow-thieving one of you. Now git!" Shannon sternly said.

The second drive, the Ellsworth Drive, was so uneventful one wondered each day when trouble would come. Grass was plentiful, water was ample and the herd, for the most part, easy to handle. Hades, however, opened its doors when the herd arrived at the Ellsworth railhead pens.

Ellsworth was the armpit of perdition. There were some one thousand permanent residents and an equal number of what one might call seekers; that is, they were seekers of anything and everything that belonged to someone else. It was a wide-open, anything-goes town; and on any given night its seventy-five professional gamblers stood in line to shear any sheep straying from the flock.

Looking over the situation, and not liking it one bit, Shannon dealt with the cattle buyers as quickly as possible. Money from the sale, except wages, was left with Wells Fargo for transfer to a Texas branch. The Bar J riders were just gathering together when gunplay erupted in the street.

The Jenkins kid, the youngest of Shannon's drovers, had been shot to pieces. The shuffling marks of his boots in the dust showed he was turned

from one side to the other by bullets slamming into his body. He looked like
a twisted scarecrow that had been used for target practice.

Funk walked up and with an awed voice said, "My God, boss, look at that.
The thong is still over the hammer of his gun. He won't hunting trouble and
he won't expecting trouble. They just shot him down emptying their guns.
As sure as rocks don't sprout wings somebody will pay for this."

A spectator whispered, "It was Addison and Gilpin. They're over in the
bar celebrating another killing. This ain't the first time this has happened."

Funk eased his gun belt around a bit and slipped the thong from the
hammer, saying, "Boss, this is my play and don't try to stop me."

"Funk, you have at it, and if you don't, I am," Shannon replied.

Shannon had seen Funk in action more than once, and he was the last
man you wanted to come against. He wasn't the fastest in the world, but he
was deadly. Few men were big enough and strong enough to handle a hogleg
like he carried. He was one of the few who still packed a holstered cap-and-
ball Colt Dragoon, weighing almost four pounds. That .44-caliber barrel
looked as big as a shotgun, and whatever that bullet hit either splintered,
splattered, or succumbed.

As Funk stepped through the swinging doors of the saloon, the would-be
bad men were bragging on gunning down the kid. Addison and Gilpin had
fancy crisscross holsters, which they probably thought made them to appear
as real gunslicks.

From day one on the drive Funk had taken a liking to Jenkins. He was
an old hand, so he took the kid under his wing. A real bond of affection had
grown between the two. Jenkins was an orphan. His daddy was killed in the
war and his momma died of the pox. He rode into the roundup camp on a
crow-bait and was hired on.

Funk stood inside the swinging door, both feet solidly planted, six feet
two of pure undiluted killing rage. There was an undertaker's look on his
face, and he spoke in a graveyard voice.

"You, two, sniveling mealy-mouthed coyotes. You gunned down one of
the finest kids that ever lived. I checked his body and you riddled him with
a least fifteen shots. He didn't even have the thong off the hammer of his
gun, but I do. Now let's see how you fare when certain death is staring you
in the face," Funk said.

Addison lunged from his chair going for his gun. It was half drawn when
Funk's gun muzzle spewed white-hot flame. Addison was slammed against
the wall as if he had been kicked by a mule. Few people, other than those
who had used such a weapon during the war, understood the power of the

.44 Dragoon.* Flipping his gun back into its holster Funk turned on Gilpin and said, "Draw your gun, you, sorry excuse for a human being. You didn't give the kid a chance. I'm giving you yours."

Funk was pushing, goading Gilpin to go for his gun. There was no giving in with him, yet he couldn't kill him in cold blood.

"Mister, look at me. I'm dropping my gun belts," Gilpin said as he reached and unbuckled his gun belt with trembling hands, and begging, "You wouldn't shoot a man who's unarmed would you?"

The cowardly ruse to save his life only increased Funk's anger. "No, I don't shoot unarmed men."

Funk thought for a moment and continued, "But there's something you really ought to know, accidents do happen."

With that he palmed that hogleg once again and shot Gilpin in the knee. He would either be on crutches the rest of his life or live with a painful gimpy leg.

"If you thought you would get off scot-free, you were mistaken," Funk said.

Turning to leave, Funk muttered, "Can't understand how that gun keeps going off when I have barely touched it."

Outside the door the crew was standing by with rifles in hand. They had already picked up Jenkins' body, wrapped it in a duster and were ready to move out.

Jenkins was given a proper burial. Words were read over him from the good book and "Big" Coop, another of the crew, who was present, lifted his voice mightily in prayer. Big Coop was one of those who believed that you could just as well pray against somebody as you could pray for them. That day Ellsworth got prayed against in a masterful way.

"Lord, you know that town is a nest of vipers, sinners doomed to the fires of Gehenna. They are the worst of your creation, if you'll pardon my saying so. I want you to bring upon them the plagues of Egypt. Let pestilence, flame, and brimstone smite them."

Coop was getting into the swing of things as he continued.

"On second thought, Lord, don't bother to call down them things or send any of your boys to do the job. In my opinion you ought to come yourself. Ride the streets on the black horse of death. Smite them hip and thigh with

---

*   Ballistics on the .44 Dragoon approximated those of the modern .44 Magnum. The shock power of its 218 grain soft-lead bullet was incredible.

your mighty sword. Slaughter them as Samson smote the Philistines. This is personal, Lord. Come upon them like Sodom and Gomorrah and don't leave nothing but corpses and ashes. Guess that's about all, Lord, I'll say good day to you and hope you will hear my prayer and do something about it! Amen."

None of the Bar J would discuss Coop's prayer, but less than two years later Ellsworth was virtually a ghost town. The Dodge City railhead had been established and herds no longer went to Ellsworth. None would say Coop's prayer had anything to do with it, but from that point on when Coop started to pray, all the boys quit what they were doing and took off their hats.

One of the hardest chores of a trail boss was contacting the family when one of the crew was killed. Funk told Shannon that the kid had a sister in Victoria, Texas, who worked as a seamstress. As the kids' personal belongings were gathered up, an address for the sister was found. A letter was written to his sister and included in it pay for the drive. Shannon felt certain she could use the money. To the man, every hand chipped in and the total amount sent was considerable.

So much for thinking about past events; at least it had helped Shannon arrive at that all-important decision. This would be his last drive for someone else. From this point on he'd drive his own cattle to market.

Two and a half weeks out of Dodge, Shannon called all the hands in for a confab. Grat, who had been with him on the Abilene and Ellsworth drives as second in command, wondered what was going on. This was the first time since starting the drive that he called all the crew in. They gathered about the chuck wagon talking among themselves. When they quieted down, Shannon spoke.

"Here's what I want you to do," he said. "I'll be leaving the drive for at least a couple of weeks. Grat's in charge. Bed 'em down here for several days. There's plenty of water and grass. Then drive easy for the pools at Pinnacle Rock. Move from Pinnacle Rock to Willow Bottoms. The grass is high and the creek running full. Hold 'em there for a few days. A week of slow driving will help fatten them up before we hit Dodge. We've been pushing mighty hard. Move from Willow Bottoms after six days. I'll join up with you a few days out of Dodge. Any questions?"

There was not a single reply. This was a group of men a man could walk the edge with. They knew their work and did it without question or hesitation. All but a couple had been with Shannon on two previous drives. What he had in mind for them would sure be a surprise.

Taking an extra horse on a lead, and saddlebags packed by Coop, Shannon hit the trail. He had to make certain that all was well at the ranch site. Between the last two drives Shannon had found his valley. Not only had the land been filed on and deeds recorded, but the historic pact with the Cheyenne renewed. No brighter future ever hovered over anyone's horizon.

Days later after crossing into the Nebraska Territory, Shannon sat his saddle, one leg looped over the horn, staring through the gap into the valley below.

The elevation at the gap must have been at least seventy-two hundred feet. Behind was a trail like a winding staircase corkscrewing its way toward snow-capped peaks partly covered by low-lying clouds. Past the lodgepole pines, about two-thirds the way up, tiny patches of snow still clung to the north side of the cliffs and tumbled boulders. Talk about being at home, that mouse-colored horse of Shannon's must have had an ounce or two of bighorn blood. Not once had he hesitated during the twisting three-mile climb to the top. If fact, he stepped out right smart as if to say, "You are in my country now."

If that horse hadn't been so mean, Shannon would have kissed him. As it was, he patted his neck and would have complimented him had he not twisted his neck around and tried to bite his hand. No one could fault him for that; it had been a punishing ride for man and beast.

Slipping from the saddle Shannon dropped the reigns and walked ahead moving through the gap. Not often in a lifetime is a man twice awed by the same vista. Before him was a scene to stagger the most overtaxed imagination. Below was a high plateau valley of lush green with two wild, tumbling streams. The twin streams sprang from either side of a lead which gently dropped from the heights to about three thousand feet. Ridges, six to eight thousand feet on either side of the valley, formed an ever-widening V as the valley disappeared into the gathering darkness. There were thousands of acres in this bit of paradise. Virgin timber graced the rising slopes; and high above, with wings flashing in the rays of a setting sun, a pair of bald eagles soared, riding the last valley updrafts of the day.

Shannon was startled out of his reverie when his horse moved up and nudged him on the shoulder. No one can ever be sure what a horse is thinking, but he seemed to say, "We're home." That was the way Shannon had felt the first time he saw the valley.

From his saddle bags Shannon slipped a pair of binoculars. Good glasses were hard to come by. These had been liberated from a burned-out wagon train he stumbled across while scouting on a cattle drive. Signs told the grim story of a swift and unexpected attack by Arapahos. Three wagons had been formed into a defensive triangle. Brass hulls, long blackened by sun and rain, littered the ground. The defenses, remnants of goods, and the rifle brass indicated the unfortunate travelers were European. About two thousand yards from the wagons were the telltale signs of a temporary Indian camp. There must have been pressing attacks, drawing fire, then swift withdrawals. This apparently happened day after day until the wagon party, weakened in numbers and without water, was overrun. The entire story was indelibly stamped upon the face of the dry waddy.

With deliberate slowness, Shannon glassed the valley below. It leaped to life through the Zeiss lens. Totally unspoiled, the valley floor teemed with life. Elk and deer, bear and beaver, even a flock of turkeys trotting ungainly through a stand of alders. High up on the slopes there were marmot and sheep. And grass, why a man could run thousands of head of cattle in the valley and barely touch its rich grass and abundant water.

Shannon's approach to the valley had been from the north. Previously he had not scouted the high country from that direction. The easier access was to the south, where some twenty to thirty miles away was the town of Stillwater. Camp was quickly made and coffee boiled. He then stretched out with cup in hand and thought of Old Jedediah Smith who had spun tales about this very place years ago. At the breaking of dawn he was out of his soogun and into the saddle. Shannon wanted to get back to the herd as soon as possible and share with the crew his proposal.

The visit to the valley had erased the last doubt in his mind concerning a shared venture with the men. Before leaving Texas he had argued with himself over what to do. He said to himself, *Self, make this your last drive. When the cattle are sold along with Logan's legacy, you could easily swing the ranching venture. You also have the investment with Adler and Company as a backup. You might as well go for the whole ten yards. It will take more than money to build the spread you envision. It will take strong men true to the brand.*

How much good fortune can a man have? As an orphan the struggle had not been overwhelming for Shannon. When hard is all a body ever had, hard didn't seem so hard. Of course along the way there had been troubling times. Yet no man makes it by himself. There's always those that give a person a hand up. In Shannon's case there were many, so far, who had gone out of their way to offer help. He had experienced many a wearying, grinding down, and threatening time of seasoning; Indian raids on the herds, bushwhacking herd cutters, stampedes, blinding snowstorms, summer heat that blistered skin and tried to cook a person's brains, choking dust, stifling sandstorms, prairie fires, rainstorms when water fell like a solid curtain of steel grey, and tornadoes destroying everything before them.

His body wounds were a human map of survival. Yet, with it all, the struggle had made Shannon stronger of body, mind, and spirit. It was the time to settle down, build that ranch, and do something, no matter how insignificant, to make the frontier a better world.

A ripe old age was not a gift of the frontier. Those who made it to the threescore and ten were few and far between. Besides, if he ever had a family he had to find that certain woman. Shannon's uncle Ted had said many a time that good women were as scarce as droppings around a rocky horse. Yet Shannon knew if he ever saw her he would know and move heaven and earth to win her heart.

One of his pa's sayings came back to Shannon. "A man," his pa said, "if he's a man, will make all the money he can, save all the money he can, and give to others all he can. If you leave any one of the three out, then they all lose worth." Shannon's plans ran along those lines and the more he thought of them, the better he liked it.

Days later Shannon caught up with the herd. Within him an excitement had grown to fever pitch. In a few more days of driving they would hit Dodge. Shannon decided it was time to throw a saddle on his dreams and ride 'em for all they were worth.

Grat held the cattle just outside Dodge while Shannon went in to deal with the buyers. They had hit the trail with some over three thousand heads, of which almost one third belonged to Shannon.

Shannon's cattle came as the result of weeks and weeks of backbreaking, bone-jarring, tooth-clenching work. Two of the present crew had worked with him driving wild cattle from the breaks along the river bottoms, almost impenetrable chaparral, and hidden canyons. These were the remnants of stampedes, fragments of herds scattered by rustlers, those abandoned after Indian attacks, or cattle left unattended during the war years. Many were old mossy backs, long in horn, mean to the core. Some were almost too big to go through a barn door. They had the most even disposition one could imagine, always nasty. They would track a man like an Apache and crush him, if possible, with brute force of hoof and horn. On the drive the semi-wild cattle had become moderately gentled being mixed with the rest of the herd. Shannon's mavericks had fattened on the trail and were in prime condition for sale.

The demand for good beef in the East had grown incredibly. Top dollar would be paid by waiting Eastern buyers, thus insuring Shannon's dream. He rode back to the cow camp with two of the most reputable buyers. After looking over the herd they offered sixteen dollars a head based on the count at the pens in Dodge. The deal was made and Shannon returned to Dodge with them, the herd trailing behind.

When the final tally was made and payments received, the men were ready to cut loose and visit the "elephant." They became a growling bunch, however, when Shannon asked them to return to camp for a meeting after which they would be paid off. None liked it. They left town with long faces, yet knowing that Shannon had a good reason for getting them out of town. It was the why that bothered them.

At the camp the crew loafed about the chuck wagon chomping at the bit to be paid off. Every saloon and bawdyhouse of Dodge was issuing its siren call, and the men were ready and willing to oblige. The ancient Greek story about lovely maidens singing their alluring songs, causing sailors to wreck their ships, couldn't hold a candle to Dodge's lure of drink and flesh. End of trail was a time of calculated rousements until wages were spent. Many were the trail herders who spent all their wages in a few nights of fast living.

There were set priorities. A new outfit of clothing was purchased. A visit to the bathhouse and the barber came next in order. For the climax, there was a bottle and a woman. Events of those few fast and glorious days would be told and retold, embellished and aggrandized, throughout the long winter in bunkhouses across the West. Not one regret, however, would be voiced.

The average puncher seldom had two coins left to rub together after the end-of-trail payday and the following revelry. Regular hands would return to the ranch as poor as Job's turkey yet would have food, shelter, and twenty-five to thirty dollars a month in wages—if they had not drawn on their pay. Those who signed on just for the drive had before them the prospect of a dreary winter of riding the grub line, looking for odd jobs to keep body and soul together. Work was hard to find and many were the lookers. At times it was all too easy for the best mother's son of them to break bad—appropriate a cow or two or even resort to armed robbery. The lone riding cowboy, who had a dollar and change in his pocket in the dead of winter, had probably been riding the hoot owl trail to survive.

The men were lined up at the rear of the chuck wagon whose drop-down table served many purposes, one of which was paymaster counter. This was an exceptional crew. Each man was fiercely independent, yet at the same time during the drive they had become amazingly interdependent. Not once had there been an uncontrolled dispute. Tempers had flared but quickly subsided. No grudges were held. Practical jokes were stock in trade for the men and broke the monotony. This was all taken in stride and good humor. Times of testing had occurred. Not once had they broken ranks. They reminded Shannon of a nest of hornets. You swat one and you have the whole swarm to deal with. He wanted this crew kept together.

Rojas was a wiry, slight-built, half-Mexican and half-Mescalero Apache. He handled the remuda and was hell on wheels with a rifle. He moved with the grace of a puma and could track a rattlesnake over rock. On his first drive Shannon had found Rojas crawling, half-crazed, along a slope above a seep. A badly broken leg, swollen and infected, was tied to his good leg with piggin strips so he could drag himself on his elbows. When Shannon rode up, Rojas looked at him through pain-glazed eyes but spoke no word. Shannon realized what had happened when he saw a horse that had been put down due to a broken leg. There was a nearby old gopher hole covered with grass. The earth all around it was churned and the edges crumbled. The horse had evidently stepped into the hole, broken its leg, and then fallen on its rider. Rojas had crawled several hundred yards to get to the water at the seep.

When Shannon lifted him, as he himself mounted his horse, Rojas's impassive face changed not a whit, yet an almost inaudible moan escaped his lips. Rojas finally recovered, after days of delirium, due to the attention of Shannon's crew. As a result Rojas developed a fierce loyalty to Shannon and the members of his crew. No one could remember if and when he had been hired. He just became one of them.

The Hatton twins were another matter. Raised up in the Nueces County on hard work and gun smoke, they were deceptively young, almost baby faced, but with plenty of frontier savvy. Theirs was a typical Texas story. Vance Hatton, their father, had a little four-by-two ranch. He and his wife Sarah were the products of hard times. Birth of the twins was the greatest thing in their lives. With a hardworking wife and two strong sons the future looked much brighter. When the twins were twelve Sarah died in childbirth. Vance and the twins buried mother and daughter on a slight rise just above their tiny ranch house. Two years later Vance was killed in a drunken brawl and the boys were on their own. They quickly acquired a bad reputation from running with the wild bunch. Shannon had read them like a book when they showed at the round up in preparation for the Ellsworth drive. They asked for work with a hangdog expression. Their outfits had become a little seedy. Hard times had come upon them, and one could tell they were having a difficult time finding honest work.

Shannon saw real possibilities in the two. He hired them on and rode them with a strong hand. As a result they turned out to be two of the most tireless, completely loyal, riders for the brand.

The old man of the bunch was Al Grat, a quiet steady hand. Yet there was a presence about him that told you he had been over the mountain and down the river, not to mention the fact that his low-slung Colt showed a powerful lot of wear. One of the crew remembered him as a former Texas Ranger. Nothing else was known of him and his former life by Shannon. He was a quiet man much given to thought. He was like a river that ran slow and deep, yet all about well knew that river had the potential of becoming a destructive flood.

Big Coop and his boy were the most respected and valuable of the lot according to the stomachs of the crew. Big Coop and Little Coop were as handy as a pocket on a shirt. Big handled a forge, hot iron, hammer and anvil with the best. Little, taught by his father, was a genius with wood and leather and could refurbish a saddle or repair boots and harness with consummate skill.

When both Coops were busy around the chuck wagon, however, it was sheer delight. They worked wonders, cooking savory stews using roots and herbs hanging in bags from the sides of the wagon. Bear sign and dried apple pie, from time to time, filled the air with their spicy scent, drawing the men to the windward to soak up the aroma. Not one dared touch until offered. Big was not to be trifled with. He stood six-three with nothing but sinew and muscle showing.

Both Big and Little would strip and wash whenever there was a river crossing, as did the rest of the men. Crisscrossing Big's back were raised bars of scars from a slave owner's whip. Both Coops had a military bearing, and others among the crew, along with Shannon, wondered if they had previously been Buffalo Soldiers. No questions were asked and no explanations required. It was irrelevant. In the West you were who you were, not what you had been.

Haskett, however, was a totally different case. Faint humor skipped around the sides of his mouth and laughter lines radiated from his eyes like crow's feet. He could always find something to be happy about and played the mouth harp like a Memphis musician. When things got serious and the dust started to fly, however, there wasn't an inch of foolishness or give in him.

On the previous drive the Allison brothers, known bad men, rode into camp one night. As always, strangers were invited to the fire and offered food and coffee by Big Coop. These two were up to no good. Haskett recognized them and immediately realized they were checking out the crew, counting guns and men. Haskett stepped from the darkness to the cookfire. It was plain to see that he had slipped the hammer thong from his gun.

He spoke quietly to the Allisons, "Jim, you and your brother Clint need to be moving on. There ain't nothing for you here unless you plan to stay sorta' permanent like." All heads turned toward the Allisons.

"Haskett! Didn't know you were with this outfit. There ain't no reason for you to get riled up," one of the Allisons said. At that, they mounted and forked out of camp like foxes with their tails on fire. From that moment on, all knew Haskett was a man to be reckoned with.

In the middle of one nooning, on Shannon's first drive, there rode up to camp a barefoot, freckled-faced, wind-blasted, sun-baked scarecrow of a boy. His pants were halfway up his legs and about five sizes too large. A piece of old halter rope served as gallowses over a shirt cut from a circle of muslin with head and arms holes. He was about as pitiful and homespun a person as could be imagined. He was all skin and bones and toothsome smile. He slipped off the back of a Missouri mule without saddle and announced, "I'm Illinois. Could I have some vittles?"

Big handed him a tin plate heaped with beef and beans. It hardly changed hands before the boy was wolfing it down. A few seconds later he was rolling on the ground in pain. His deprived, shrunken stomach couldn't take it.

That's how an Illinois ploughboy joined the crew. He had been with the spread since that night. Most all the green had worn off him in the past few years. He liked the cowboy life yet constantly seemed to yearn for farming days.

Rounding out the group was Ruble and Funk. Both were the quiet type yet would hurrah with the best of them on occasion. Both knew cows, worked hard, and pulled more than their weight when there were hard, grubby, sweat-popping tasks. It was rumored about the camp that Ruble was as good with a rifle as Rojas and that Funk had a military background of which he seldom, if ever, spoke.

One night Shannon noticed Funk on the fringe of the fire, cleaning a strange-looking gun. Yet it was one he, not the others, recognized. His pa had brought such a gun from the war. Somehow he had held on to his as a link to the past until the Cheyenne raid on the freight train. Funk was swift and deft as he handled the piece. Few men in the West owned a LeMat. Funk carefully wrapped and returned the pistol to his saddlebags. It was rumored knowledge that Jeb Stuart, as well as some of his boys, carried LeMat revolvers. Shannon said nothing but along with the way Funk took care of his horses, it caused him to suspect that Funk may have had cavalry seasoning during the war.

Looking up from the tailgate into the eyes and faces of the men Shannon knew the decision he would announce was the right one. It was time to call the crew together and set before them his proposition.

"We've all been together on three drives," Shannon began. "Drives that forced from a man his best or his worst. You have shown me only the best. I've a proposition to put to you. This is my last trail drive for someone else. Within a few weeks I'll begin building my own ranch. The land is already filed on. It is a bit remote, in the high mountains, some forty to fifty miles from the nearest town, and is in Cheyenne territory. I've had a long standing relationship with them and the ranch will not be troubled."

Something clicked in Grat's mind at the mention of a special relationship with the Cheyenne. He cleared his throat before he interrupted. "Boss, you wouldn't be kin to Irish Murphy would you? There must be some almighty good reason for the Cheyenne to let someone run cows on their holdings."

"Irish Murphy was my grandfather and married to Little Fawn, daughter of Yellow Sky, a Cheyenne chieftain. I have Cheyenne blood in my veins and rightly proud of it," Shannon explained.

"No offense meant, boss, but there's not many this side of the Ohio who have not heard the story of Irish Murphy and the white buffalo. If this ain't the dangest thing. Never would have thought it. Why, your grandpa is a legend," Grat said.

"Getting back to what I was saying," Shannon continued. "From Mr. Brinkly, the herd owner, I have bought the remuda, chuck and supply wagons all absolutely necessary to speed up the plans I have.

"Every one of you wonders what will happen when you're too old, or stove up, or sick to stay on the hurricane deck. If I am to build a ranch, I've got to have men. Men, who will fight for the brand, work for the brand, and be loyal to the brand no matter what. Every last one of you is such a man."

They all looked shocked and surprised. This was the longest speech he'd made to the men. What was more surprising he hadn't begun to talk. In turn, Shannon looked at each of the men.

"Rojas," Shannon said, "I'd like you to stay on in charge of the remuda for all drives as well as building the breeding herd. I like the way you break a horse, gentling it rather than trying to destroy its spirit. One day soon we'll talk about a breeding effort to produce the best cow horses in the West.

"Coop, I'll sorely need you and your son. You'll be over the smithy and the tack room, as well as the kitchen. You'll have extra help in the kitchen. More friends will be made for us around your table than can be made by a tooth doctor who pulls teeth without pain. But I have one request. Lighten up a bit on the coffee. I like it strong, but I do hate to cut it off like a plug of tobacco and chew it."

Coop just smiled his monstrous smile and with a twinkle in his eye said, "Children like you shouldn't fool with coffee no way!"

When the laughter ceased, Shannon continued, "Al, I want you as range foreman, if you'll sign on. No one has more cow and range savvy than you. We need to set up line shacks, locate waterholes, select spots for cofferdams, and pick the best high meadows for haying. You know the drill better than I."

Pausing for a minute he looked over the group. The Hatton twins were in the back shuffling their feet while at the far side was Haskett, Illinois, Funk, and Ruble. Haskett stood ill at ease. Illinois had question marks in his eyes. Funk and Ruble looked like two granite statues showing no emotion except for a stern set of the jaws. Doubtless they were wondering if they were going to be included. Those already mentioned would have steady jobs. Those not singled out by Shannon would be staring a cold hard winter in the face.

Turning, Shannon looked at the Hatton twins who favored one another but were not identical. One stood over six feet while the other hit about five-seven. Shortly after joining the crew the men started calling them "Dap" and "Gin." Their nicknames, thanks be to a guardian angel, had stuck. Their real first names were Virgil and Virginius. Every time those given names became known in a saloon or bawdyhouse there was first laughter, then disparaging remarks resulting in head-to-head confrontations and near riots.

"You, two, are the youngest in the outfit in years but have shown you know cows, the range, and are not afraid of hard work. I'd like you to be the backbone of our range riders. As the herds grow we'll pitch in and help. At roundup we'll put on extra hands for the gather, the branding, and the drive," Shannon told the Hatton twins.

"As for you Illinois," Shannon said, "you keep on talking with a burning passion about that farm back home. At times you sound sorta' homesick for sticking a plow in the ground and producing a crop. Well, I want our ranch to be self-sufficient, a regular homestead. We'll need grain crops, an orchard, and a kitchen garden, plus what needs to be put up for the winter. If you think you can handle it, you've got a permanent place with the rest of us. I figure if you are going to eat as much as you do, you'll produce plenty for the sake of self-preservation, if for no other reason."

"Boss, I don't eat so much. Just enough for a growing boy!" Illinois replied. When the friendly banter died down, Big calmly remarked, "I'd rather feed ten hungry grub line riders in January than one young fellow with a growing appetite who don't know when to say enough!"

Funk and Ruble stood side by side across the cookfire. These two had sided in the first drive and had welded a friendship closer than most brothers. They each recognized in the other that certain quality of quiet strength. They were a couple of warriors, tested in battle Shannon suspected, and probably scarred of body and emotion. It was evident each had some formal education capped with an abundance of native intelligence. There was never a brag, never a threat, never an angry word from them. Yet they possessed a wariness like that of a hunted animal which could, if necessary, turn into a maelstrom of fury. Each had military bearing, and their eyes told the story of incredible suffering and loss. They could be of critical importance to the success of the proposed venture.

"Funk, I'm asking you, Ruble, and, Haskett, to take on an all-important responsibility, that of the inside operations of the ranch. Above all the protection and defense of the entire ranch. There's been rumors about trouble in the area where we will set up operations. To what extent or what kind of trouble I do not know at this point. The word I have gotten is that a big outfit has moved in and wants to control all of the range that borders theirs or is even near them. From all I can observe, none of you were idle during the war. You sit your saddles like cavalrymen and have the manners and bearing of command. I need you and want you to stay on."

For a moment Shannon was silent. Then he continued with deep emotion clearly shown by saying, "I'm not a wishful man, not much of a praying man, but I pray and hope all of you will stick with me. You're a shining crew."

It was time to come to the most important part of the proposal. Shannon proceeded, "If you will stay, you'll all receive for the first year thirty a month and found. On the first of each New Year for three years the pay will increase by five dollars a month that is as we say back in the mountains, 'Mother Nature willing and the cliffs don't fall.' Now, last and probably most important, if you sign on, you will become lifetime partners in the ranch. Twenty percent of the ranch profits each year will be split evenly among you. You have a lifetime right to bunk and board. Pick your place in the bunkhouse and at the table and it's yours all the way through the rocking chair days. Should you choose to leave after a few years then we'll try to buy out your percentage. Sleep on it and in the morning give me your decision. Remember one thing, however, you'll not only ride for the brand, you will own a piece of the Bar J brand."

As the men began to saddle up for the ride into town, Big Coop walked up and said, "Boss, I don't rightly know how to ask this, and I surely don't want to put you out or ask for too much. You've been awfully good to the boy and me. Now you offer us more than we ever dreamed to have. I have a deep sadness inside. It's a longing and a yearning so bodacious it can't be put in words. I haven't seen my Mandy; she's my wife, in more than four years. When I sorta' left the army, she stayed behind. To tell the truth, I left sudden like. Had a set to with the sutler on post. He was from the deep South, former plantation owner, who took his pick of the women slaves. Thought he could do the same with my Mandy. Left him about a foot short of life. Won't nothing left to do but run. When he tried to force my Mandy, I lost control. At the time I was in the Tenth Calvary formed at Fort Leavenworth by Col. Benjamin Grierson, and Little Coop was with the Ninth Calvary. My Mandy she worked on what we called 'Soap Suds Row.' The army allowed four laundresses per company. They were usually the wives, widows, or friends, if you know what I mean, of the enlisted men. Between Mandy and me we had it good until the incident. Little Coop joined with me in deserting. We headed for Texas and started cooking for trail drives.*

"Now, Mandy girl can cook better than me. She can wash and keep house. She'd be mighty fine to have around the ranch. She wouldn't be no bother and a lotta' help. And Little Coop, as old as he is, needs his momma's gentling. He misses her something awful."

The look on Big Coop's face was unforgettable. Fear and hope, entreaty and doubt, humbleness and pride shone through his eyes and were reflected in every word spoken.

"Coop, you are a good man and an honest man," Shannon said. "You send for your Mandy, and as soon as possible we'll build a place for the three of you. But for the time being, you will have to live under the stars with the rest of us."

Coop turned and walked away wiping a tear with the back of his hand. What else could Shannon have said? If Mandy was a better cook than Big Coop and the crew found out he hadn't sent for her, they would have lynched him.

---

* The practice of hired laundresses was adopted by the United States Army in 1802 from the British Army. They were the only women recognized by army regulations and granted privileges such as health care. Their set pay for laundry was $0.50 per month for enlisted men, $2.00 per month for single officers, $4.00 per month for married officers and an additional amount for officers' children and servants.

Quietness settled on the camp. All of the crew had gone into town to celebrate. Overhead a canopy of stars spangled the night with their brilliance. A low burning fire cast the glow of its coals against the chuck wagon causing dancing shadows to chase one another. Lying on his soogun, saddle for a pillow, dreams of the future filled Shannon's head.

Dreams are strange things. At first they can be as fleeting as a will-o'-the-wisp, just mere shadows. They could be made real, but it took a lot of doing. Yet that was happening all over the West. It was more than a westward movement of people; it was a migration of dreams.

From the raped plantations and farms of the South and from the stench of the disadvantaged poverty-stricken slums, masses turned to the West. European immigrants of low estate and importunates of high station along with the suppressed legions of China came seeking their destiny. Members of England's landed gentry, ostracized nobility from the courts of Europe, and investors hungry for property and profits poured into the frontier.

Among them were found those who would turn the dreams of the little man to dust. They were the power brokers—land barons, railroad scions, investment bankers, and shipping magnates whose sole mission was to reap the huge profits available to those who were ruthless enough to acquire them. They were persons of rank, power, influence, and wealth, who carefully compartmentalized their lives, never permitting ethics to influence their businesses.

The saddest stories of life are written not when big dreams conflict with big dreams, but when the small dreams of honest simple folk are challenged by the big dreams of the powerful. Then every hope of the economically, politically, or socially disadvantaged is crushed in the juggernaut of greed.

Dreams have always been the stuff of life. At first, just fleeting thoughts, nebulous with no body. At first abstract, yet as time passes a semblance of shape and substance occur. Finally in a burst of creativity they solidify. The imagined, and intangible, takes form in the mind; and the dream is ready to be made into a concrete reality.

It is one thing to have a dream, it is another to have the courage and discipline to flesh it out. To the plains Indians, dreams were windows of the soul through which one saw the hopes of the inner being. They were there to challenge heart, mind, and spirit.

Shannon's dream stood before him, and no matter what the odds were against it, he intended to grasp that dream and fulfill its meaning for his life and that of his friends.

As his musing continued there was the far off drumming of hoof beats. No one in their right mind would push a horse that hard at night unless on an urgent mission, thought Shannon.

Al Grat raced into camp. Slid from the saddle. His voice shook with anger. "There's trouble in town. Little Coop has been hurt and shamed. The marshal has jailed the crew. I stopped by the barber's to get a bath and a shave. The boys went on to the nearest saloon. Fellow came in the barber shop telling what happened so I burned leather to get you."

Saddling Shannon's hammer-headed roan never was an easy job. This time not a muscle moved as he threw on the blanket and saddle, then slipped the bit in his mouth. Horses are the dangest things. Sometimes they sense urgency or need.

Mounting he yelled at Al, "Tell me about it as we ride. I want to sort this thing out before going off half-cocked."

By the time the outskirts of Dodge were hit, Shannon had the whole story. All the men except Al had gone to the Palace Saloon. Another trail crew, one from the Slash L, was at the bar. Some of the Bar J boys were jawing about starting up the new ranch. When one mentioned its location as being somewhere in the vicinity of Stillwater, a small war started.

The Slash L foreman, man by the name of Norton, let it be known in no uncertain terms there wasn't room for another spread in that part of the country. Plus, he added, "The colonel would tolerate no outfit that hired buffalo boys."

Little Coop, not willing to let the insult go unanswered started for Norton when four of the Slash L boys came up from a card table with drawn guns. Shannon's boys had checked their guns like the posted laws of Dodge required. There wasn't anything they could do to stop Norton and his men from downing Little Coop and notching his ears with a bowie knife.

There was only one horse at the hitching rail in front of the marshal's office. Grat and Shannon stepped down and walked through the office door. The look on Shannon's face indicated he was in no mood for small talk.

"Marshal, I'm Murphy and this is Al Grat." Before another word could be spoken, Thompson exclaimed, "Thunderation! Al Grat. Why, man I haven't set eyes on you since Beeville when you quit riding for Wells Fargo and joined the Texas Rangers."

Al was as surprised as the marshal. Abel Thompson and Grat went back a long ways when they both, in younger and more reckless years, rode the hoot owl trail.

"Didn't know you were in these parts, Abel, but right now you've got a king-size problem on your hands," Grat said.

Breaking in, Shannon firmly summed up the situation, saying, "We are law-abiding folk who believe the law applies equally to all people. There are certain things I want to know, and I want to know them right now. One, how much is the fine levied on my men? Two, why were Slash L riders armed? Three, why haven't you arrested the Slash L foreman for assault with a deadly weapon? Four, why aren't the Slash L riders in jail for uttering threats, reckless endangerment, and harassing law-abiding businessmen in Dodge? My men had checked their guns as you well know."

Thompson was shaken by the blunt words. Such words he had only heard from lawyers and judges. He was angry and uncertain how to reply. One thing he knew, however, he was not dealing with some unlettered range boss. Those long hours of instruction by Waldroop on the keelboat and the hours of reading Blackstone since that time were standing Shannon in good stead.*

"You have to understand," Abel replied, "the Slash L brings a herd in every year. Their trail crew at times numbers about thirty. When paid off, they come into town and spend their money. The local businessmen, those who run the town, expect me to cut them a little slack."

"Abel, you listen to me," Shannon said sternly. "I'm not going to say this but once. I can't abide a lawman who waffles in his talk and betrays the badge for the sake of a job. Here's two hundred dollars, more than enough for the fines you are illegally imposing on my crew. Write a receipt and sign it. Then open those cell doors and return my men's guns. Next go home, close the door and go to bed."

Thompson's hand began to move almost imperceptibly toward the butt of his gun, and Al exclaimed, "Abel, for heaven's sake don't try it! He told you his name is Murphy, but he's known as Shannon."

Shannon! Among the legendary names of all the fast guns, the deadliest of the lot was a shadowy figure, one who moved about the darkened stage of western lore. Shannon was like some fictional character in a folk tale. He was and he wasn't. Like a shell game, now you see him now you don't. Yet whenever there was left in ruins the designs of some pompous, evil, grasping,

---

*   Sir William Blackstone's *Commentaries on the Laws of England* published in four volumes between 1765-1769 were formative for the legal profession and the teaching of law in England and the United States.

malignant individual who had a sudden demise, Shannon was suspected. His very nature was that of the protector of the downtrodden, the disadvantaged, the outcast, the struggler.

Shannon never set himself up as a gunman and rarely, if ever, was in conflict with the law. Seldom was he accused of riding with the wild bunch. They all had heard of him and planned to steer clear of his six-gun magic. Few men could match his mastery of gun fighting, and it was doubtful anyone was superior to him.

From one end of the West to the other there were many fast guns. By face or name, they were known by every sheriff, marshal, bartender, gambler, ranch owner, and cowpoke. For each, such one, there were others as swift, accurate, and deadly with a six-gun as those who were in the limelight. They seldom drew against another man but when they did, it was in self-defense.

The legendary stories of Shannon's gun handling started in Natchez. "Natchez-under-the-Hill" was considered by most as a hop, skip, and jump below Sodom and Gomorrah; a hellish environment of adventurers, prostitutes, gamblers, and cutthroats. This brotherhood of thievery victimized any unwary traveler and contested with each other using fist, knife, and gun.

Shooting matches for high and low stakes were a daily occurrence, with the favorite target a swinging bottle. Five men would toe the line. Five bottles would be put in motion thirty feet away. On the count of three all would draw and fire. The first bottle broken won the pot into which each shooter anted up fifty cents. According to the story, a young keelboater, maybe fifteen years old walked up, dropped his half-dollar in the pot, and eased an old .36 Remington around his hip. Four shots later the kid had picked up eight dollars. He had won each time.

According to a short piece in the *Mississippi Herald* under the heading, "Kid Gives Shooting Lessons"; it all happened this way. When the youngster started to leave he grinned and said, "Mighty neighborly of you to let me shoot. I'd stay on but I don't have enough caps, powder, and ball but for four loads." The story went on to tell that one of the river rats who had lost palmed a knife and started for the boy. Seems he looked him square in the face and let him know that if he didn't drop the knife, he would kill him. "With what?" came the reply." Mister, do you think I am dumb enough to be around this crowd and not save a load in my gun?" The outdone loser dropped the knife by his side and in the same motion went for his gun. He was dead before he cleared leather. The kid disappeared in the crowd.

Another story made the round of cow camps across the West. A young cowhand was stopped on the streets of Salina, Kansas, taunted and bullied by

Forgas, a local gunslick who was slightly drunk and on the prowl. Drunk or sober he was greased lightning with a wheel gun. The youngster gave Forgas a long look of contempt and in a quiet, almost inaudible voice, said, "I've had enough of you. Touch your gun and I'll kill you." Forgas reached but his hand had barely moved when he froze. Sweat popped out on his brow. He was staring into the muzzle of a .44/40 Colt that seemed to have suddenly materialized. Forgas unbuckled his gun belt, let it drop in the street, and walked away from the fight and the grave.

An old timer sitting propped in a chair in front of the hotel remarked, "You know, that fellow reminds me of a boy I saw in a shooting match back on the Trace."

Along the outlaw trail other stories were told of a gunman with a mystical flashing draw, uncanny accuracy, and split-second reflexes. Hernando Vasquez, a border gunfighter with a solid reputation for shoot-out savvy and steel nerves had been the survivor of more than a few gun battles. He had seen a gunman unknown to him in an El Paso showdown. Rod Sodaman, a vicious killer with a sadistic nature, was beating a young cowhand unmercifully, when a stranger stepped in and separated them.

According to Vasquez, only a few words were spoken to the effect that the young cowhand's intent was to tear Sodaman limb from limb. If there was anything left over, he would be fed to the buzzards since not even a coyote would touch the remains. Sodaman reached for his gun but was dead before it cleared leather. What sounded like one shot was actually two. Both of them centered in the left-hand pocket of Sodaman's shirt.

Vasquez later told at the bar that he shuddered as if somebody had stepped on his grave, saying, "If I ever saw death, it was in his eyes. I'd hang up my guns before I would brace that man."

Thompson had not only heard these stories but many others. To contend with Shannon's guns was a sure invitation to an early demise. Common sense in making the decision before him was to the lawman the only route to self-preservation. He was getting on in years and the prospect of a few golden days, as an ex-lawman, appealed to him at the moment. Swallowing his pride and controlling his anger Thompson accepted payment of the fines, wrote a receipt, handed the cell keys to Shannon, and walked out the door, putting his hat on. Halfway down the street, he paused, leaning against a building due to a sudden weakness. The thought gripped him that this could and would have been the last night of his life had he not given in to the demands of Shannon. Thompson trembled. Death had lurked behind Shannon's every word. It was not a good night for dying.

With signed receipt in hand, Shannon asked the boys to return to camp, but Al, Ruble, and Funk bucked, insisting that they ought to be in on whatever was going to happen. Shannon turned and started crossing the street toward the saloon. The rest of the crew simply stood there, all of the same mind. They were staying and backing Shannon's play no matter what might occur.

As silently as a faint breeze Shannon slid through the open saloon door, took one step to the left, and paused for a moment to let his eyes adjust to the light. Then he stepped to the center of the entranceway.

The rage churning within had turned into a lust for battle. A dead calm settled over Shannon. He was ready.

"Norton," Shannon's voice cracked with authority, "on your feet. I'm going to read to you from the book of Colt, chapter 44, verse 40. You are a mean little man, not worth the powder it takes to send you to the grave. You marked one of my men. You said there was not room for another spread around Stillwater. Now you listen and listen well. If you or anyone of the Slash L outfit ever again comes against me or mine, threatens my crew, or even look wrong in our direction, you'll answer to me."

Norton came to his feet with a roar, turning over his chair, and upsetting the table. Cards, whiskey, glasses, and money flew in every direction.

Shannon looked at Norton with undertaker eyes, cold and black like frozen swamp water. Norton went sick inside. His blood chilled. Tiny tremors coursed through his body. In his mind a warning alarm screamed its message of death. He had never feared man or beast but this was different. There was something about this man, which reminded him of an open grave beckoning him. In him was no mercy, no forgiving, not letting up.

"Unbuckle your gun belt, Norton," Shannon ordered. "Let it drop on the floor. The rest of you do the same."

"The devil we will," Norton said. "We're eight guns to your one." In the split second of silence that followed, in each door and window of the saloon there were the audible clicks of Colt and Winchester hammers being eared back. Shannon's crew was taking their part in the play.

"Norton, you hit the saddle and ride," Shannon yelled. "They tell me California is right nice this time of year. Don't ever let me lay eyes on you again for if I do, I'll drop you where you stand. Don't speak one word. Take what you have and git. Leave now for parts unknown or a shallow grave, the choice is yours.

"As for the rest of you, carry this message to the colonel, whoever he is. Tell him I am building my ranch. If he or any of his men come against me, I'll smash him. And, if he wants to know who I am, there are people who know me as Shannon."

As the crew rode slowly back to the camp they were filled with excitement. They had recognized all along their boss was no run-of-the-mill cowhand who, like hundreds of others, knew how to handle men and cows and worked hard at it. The accounts of such men were common fare around bunkhouses, line shacks, and cook fires.

Each one of Shannon's riders, without the knowledge of the others, made a decision at that moment to accept partnership in the ranching venture. They would ride with him for their brand. Shannon's given word was rock hard and steel strong. It could be taken to the bank for deposit or withdrawal. He was a man's man and each was proud to partner with him.

CHAPTER 7

Lost Love

Six months had passed since they left Dodge and arrived at the ranch site. Two freight wagons, plus four Conestoga wagons, loaded with provisions and the basic necessities of furnishings, as well as the remuda, finally made it without incident. Then the work started. They were creating a home, betting on the future with combined skills and commitment.

Three weeks after arrival at the ranch site the Hatton twins and Haskett rode in driving fifty head of mixed Hereford stock with two strong bulls, the herd's beginning. They milled a bit and settled in, grazing on the knee-deep grass of the high mountain valley. They too had found a new home.

The main room of the ranch house along with the kitchen and bedroom were dried in within weeks while across the way the bunkhouse was completed. Stable and corrals anchored a corner of the compound. Springs had been cleaned, coffer dams built to catch runoff rainwater; a gusher of a spring was diverted by a raceway to supply the ranch house and garden; locations for line shacks had been chosen and meadows for haying selected. Smoke rose from the chimneys of kitchen and forge. About the table talk was that of men proud of their accomplishments and plans for the future. Such a closeness had developed between the men it was now more of a family than a ranch crew.

Had Shannon not been mountain-bred, the buildings would have been raised quicker. Homestead buildings in the Smokies were built to last for generations. Log construction had been developed to the point of a fine art by the homespun craftsman. In the low country, the coastal area, cabins had been built of round logs with a simple saddle notch for the corners. Oftentimes there was no squaring of the timbers but when they did, it was only top and bottom.

Mountain folk, with an abundance of giant trees available, built with squared logs. Shannon and the Coops squared the felled logs with broad axe and adze, dovetailing the corner notches creating a joint that was strong, stable, and virtually airtight. Foundation logs and floor joists were placed on stone bases to sustain the weight of the walls and puncheon floors. Froe and mallet in the hands of Funk and Ruble turned out a mound of shakes for the roofs. When completed the complex resembled a Smoky Mountain homestead built to last.

It was time to let the town of Stillwater know that the Bar J had indeed settled in the area. On the way to the ranch site they had avoided the town, circling for miles in order not to attract attention. Between the ranch and town were thirty miles, as the crow flies, of isolation. Since everything had been packed in, only rumors of a new spread had reached town.

Shannon approached Stillwater in early morning light. Screened by blue spruce trees on the east slope Shannon began to glass the town and valley below. He wanted to watch the town come to life and observe its activities for one full day. This way of reading a town was taught to him by a former bank robber turned buffalo hunter. Shannon had sided with him to hunt buffalo during an off season from trail driving.

Below was a rocky incline ending on a pebbly bench beside the creek. Freshets had left sloping terraces to ever-widening banks as the stream flowed under a heavy post and beam bridge. Beyond the edge of the town the stream narrowed again, and the water leaped and swirled among rocks in a rapid.

A methodical glassing of the town began. Before reaching the bridge, there were a number of shacks, a bar, and what appeared to be a bawdyhouse. Just across the bridge was a sizeable livery. Beside it the blacksmith was stoking up the forge for the day ahead.

To the east of the street, false front buildings were interspersed with those of stone and brick. Reuter's Bank stood two stories high, flanked by Leiberman's Mercantile and Altman's Hardware. Anchoring either end of the row of businesses were saloons: the Imperial and Palace.

For hours before riding upstream, Shannon watched the town come to life and then settle into its customary daily routine. The next morning he crossed the stream and found a spot from which he could determine the nature of the west side of the street. Shannon again settled down with the glasses. He scanned, foot by foot, the west side. In the center was a two-story hotel, the Windsor House, with upper and lower porch. To the right of the hotel was a millenary shop, a dry goods store, a hardware, a barbershop, a newsstand, a gunsmith's shop, a café, a Wells Fargo office, and a stage station with outside stairs leading up to a doctor's and attorney's offices. At the south end of the town was a schoolhouse and a church. The town looked solid and permanent, quite prosperous.

One scene above all others elicited Shannon's attention and completely intrigued him. On the stone-slab steps before the schoolhouse door stood the teacher furiously ringing a bell, calling the children to line up. The normal pushing and shoving was going on to be first in line. Suddenly a fight broke out between two of the boys, one three times the size of the other, in fact he was larger than the teacher. Shannon grinned and thought, *There's one in every crowd, no matter where it is.*

The smaller of the two boys was a fiery redheaded little squirt, who attacked his bullying opponent with pent-up fury and flying fists. The older boy just reared back and clobbered the little fellow. Blood flew from his nose or split lip. Shannon couldn't tell which. Heedless of the blow and the pain, the redhead flew into the bully landing more than one telling blow.

As the teacher parted them, the bully, having totally lost his temper, swung at the teacher. What happened next was the likes of which Shannon had never seen in his life. The teacher as calmly and as deftly as a bull fighter blocked the swing and grabbing the boy's arm twirled him around and slammed him head on into the side of the school house. Then she took the hand of the feisty redhead and led the other children into the school. At the end of the line was the bully, shaking his head, and probably wondering what had happened to him. Now that's a woman to ride over the mountain with, thought Shannon.

Late in the afternoon a group of riders rode into town from the south. It was a hard-looking crowd. One thing was for certain, they weren't thirty-a-month ranch hands. Each was well mounted, much better than the average rider. Harness and saddle were high dollar—several with silver conches, which glittered in the sun. Such display of swell-headed vanity would quickly invite death from hostiles. Their flashes in the sun would reveal the presence of the rider for miles. Each had a Winchester in a scabbard, and most wore tied-down holsters. These were paid warriors, hired guns, who rode for pay, not for pride in the brand.

But why? The town and the countryside appeared peaceful. Before filing on the land, Shannon had investigated the history of the town. In fact, through Wells Fargo discrete inquiries had been made.

South of town there was a large ranch running some twenty-five to thirty thousand head. Also south there had been two small spreads. Some panning for gold was carried on with no big strikes. Unique were two freeholds granted to a couple of settlers who had nursed Abner Lusk, the town's founder, through a bout with smallpox. In gratitude each had been given one hundred sixty acres from Lusk's holdings next to the town. Both of the free holders were German immigrant farmers.

Erlich and Gottwald irrigated their fields from the ample waters of the creek producing much-needed grain and an abundance of vegetables, both of which were in short supply and extremely costly when brought in by wagon freight.

Erlich also raised hogs. Cured side meat was a staple of western diet when available. It was in incredible demand. Range hands would joke with Erlich, calling him a "hog slopper." He'd only laugh and in his usual jovial manner would reply, "Ya, I raise the pigs. The pigs become hogs. The hogs become side meat and ham. You tease. I am sad all way to the bank to put in your money. Pretty good joke, ya!"

Something about the group that had ridden in troubled Shannon. One or two of the riders seemed familiar. Even with the glasses he could not see their facial features clearly. There was only time for a fleeting look before they dismounted and turned to enter a saloon. Nevertheless, a tiny warning bell rang in his mind. He thought, *Perhaps it would come to me later.* For some reason Shannon connected them with an event in the past but could not recall the particulars.

The day grew late. Shannon rolled up his blanket and finished chewing a strip of jerky. He fell asleep thinking of the business to be taken care of on the morrow. Some of the boys were to ride in with pack mules and wagons. It was time to stock up for the weeks ahead. In the morning, however, it would be first things first: a room, a bath, new clothes, and a good meal.

If ever anyone looked like the backside of hard luck, Shannon did as he rode into town. Most of the fringe was gone from his deerskin tunic. Elbows showed through each sleeve. There were black half circles of sweat stains on chest and sides. At places the buckskin was split. Across the back were two lines of stitching and one across the chest. The leather along each seam was dark, rusty brown, which spoke of dried blood and knife slashes. Buckskin trousers and high-laced moccasins looked worse, if that was possible. One leg was split, both in tatters at the bottom, while the moccasins were little more than scraps of leather held together by repairs. Thus, he looked when entering the Emporium, Leiberman's mercantile.

"There's some things I need," he called into the dim interior of the store, not seeing a clerk in sight. Leiberman slowly rose from behind the counter. He looked at Shannon with piercing eyes and grimacing face. Then, with a smile in his voice, he spoke. "If I was you, I'd start with a bath and a shave.

Then I'd burn those clothes as an act of mercy and compassion for your fellowmen."

Some folks a fellow immediately dislikes the minute he rubs up against them. There are others whose open honesty and plain words couched in semijest appeal to a man's best responses. An immediate liking built within Shannon for Leiberman. Shannon chuckled, "Lay me out a couple of changes of clothes from bottom to top. Plain tough working clothes are what I need. Also throw in another outfit of the very best. There's a lot more to get after I clean up and rest a bit."

"You might try the Windsor House, clean rooms and the best food to be had for a hundred miles. There's one thing that bothers me just a trifle. Son, you don't look like you got two dollars to howdy each other," Leiberman dubiously asked.

"I wouldn't want you to lose your sleep tonight, friend, worrying about my financial condition," Shannon replied.

Shannon slipped his fingers inside the waistband of his pants. Taking out three fifty-dollar gold pieces, he put them down one by one on the counter, saying, "Mr. Storekeep, don't let appearances fool you too much. Just put that on the books. I'll draw against the account tomorrow."

Leiberman's eyes widened when he saw the gold pieces and said, "Friend, be careful how you show that kind of money around here! There's some of that Slash L crew that would dry gulch you for half that, believing there was a lot more."

"You let me worry about that," Shannon replied. "You worry about my three accounts. These three gold pieces. First on the account of the fact that I'll need a lot of supplies. Two, on account I believe I can trust you. And the third account, if you are not straight with me, I'll come over here and tear this store down board by board."

All of this Shannon said in good humor and with a grin on his face. Leiberman stuck his hand across the counter to shake hands, saying, "Son, we can do business together." He had a grip of steel and in his clear blue eyes was the look of a man who had not always stood behind the counter of a store selling everything from guns to ribbons. He would be a good man to call friend.

Moving from the store's dim light into the full sunlight outside caused Shannon to blink a time or two as he looked up and down the dusty street.

Totally without warning it happened. The whole world grew still. Shannon took in a deep slow breath. Across the street stood a woman of breathtaking beauty. It was the schoolteacher he had watched when checking the town. There was about her a soft feminine grace with not a hint of anything but sheer perfection. Statuesquely she paused looking across the street. Their eyes met. Shannon's being seemed to skip a beat. He could see the tiny laughter wrinkles at the corner of her deep blue eyes. A hint of interested amusement played about her mouth and full lips as she noticed his shabby appearance. She returned his gaze boldly without the slightest hint of flirtation.

Little did Shannon know, but fervently hoped, that she shared something of his instant reaction. Was this ever a woman to ride over the mountain with! You could tell she was proud to be what she was without a bit of pretense. She was not reluctant to greet the truly complimentary look of men in general and this one in particular. A lecherous stare would have been met with a withering glance of contempt. This was a lot of woman, and she knew it without any display or coquettishness.

Shannon was dazed by the encounter, reacting like a schoolboy. He took only one step forward, forgetting he stood on the plank store porch, and fell sprawling into the dusty street with packages flying in every direction.

Looking up, he saw her standing there, hand to mouth trying to stifle her laughter. The Irish in him rose to the occasion.

"You can truthfully say that when I fall for a beautiful lady, I go all the way," Shannon said. "By the way, if you aren't taken or spoken for, then I'm coming calling in dead earnest." With that he scrambled to his feet, picked up the packages, and headed for the Windsor House.

Before entering the store Shannon noticed a group of hard cases standing in front of the saloon across the way. Scarcely could he have imagined what would next occur.

Two riders, one on either side of the street rode past. Silently two lasso loops slipped over his shoulders. Jerked from his feet, they began to drag him up and down the street. Covering his head with his arms as best he could did little good. On the second round they skidded him into a hitching post. Shooting stars burst in his head. Then a brief blackout washed over him. Within minutes, however, he was fully conscious.

Crawling to a horse trough he plunged his head into the water. Looking up he saw no one in sight nearby. The water washed the cobwebs out of his mind, but it did not erase the picture of the two men who dragged him. Picking up his packages he headed to the hotel. He thought, *Why did no one come to my aid?*

Within Shannon there was a building fury that he knew would soon turn into a deadly calm resolve. The cry of the ancient gods of war coursed through his brain. They could only be quieted by righting of the wrong.

The room clerk took one look at Shannon and knew it was the better part of wisdom to accede to his wishes without any questions. On the counter he placed the money for a week's stay, signed the register, and took the offered key. Turning to go, he ordered water for bathing and requested that the new clothes be pressed and returned within the hour.

All who saw Shannon step into the street from the hotel could tell they were looking at a different man. Yet little could they know what he was thinking. Two courses of action were fixed like granite in his mind. First, find the men who had done the dragging. Second, find out as much as possible about the girl.

Along with the resolves were questions. What was wrong with the town? No one had come to his assistance either when dragged or afterward when he was lying dazed and briefly unconscious in the street. Had the girl witnessed what happened? If so, how did she react? Had someone ordered the attack or were the men who dragged him just plain mean? What was it about two of the men at the saloon hitching rail that reminded him of something out of his past? Shannon intended to get some answers one way or another. If anyone got in his way, then it would be their misfortune.

Nestling between Shannon's shoulder blades, beneath his shirt, was "Whispering Death," the double-edged throwing knife shaped from one piece of Damascus steel. Only the blade makers of Damascus and Toledo originally knew its secrets—secrets they had learned during the Arab and Berber incursions during the eighth century. Such blades were unmatched in balance, flexibility, and razor-sharpness. In the hands of an expert thrower they were as swift and deadly as a horned viper. None had mastered its use better than Shannon. Since first being taught by Rom, he too had perfected the art.

Against his hip a Colt .44/40 rested ever so easily in its hand fitted holster. Hours of practice, drawing and firing, had convinced Shannon that the smoother the release of the gun from leather, the quicker and surer the draw.

A Mexican saddlemaker in Tascocas had constructed the holster of unusually heavy leather, double back with single front. Once in Shannon's hands, work began to form the outer layer to fit every contour of the Colt.

As a boy he had watched the Cherokees soften leather strips with water or steam and attach spearheads or axe heads to shafts with such bindings. The wet leather would then be rubbed with a piece of antler or smooth stone as it was drying, fitting every contour of shaft and stone.

Painstakingly, hour after hour, the holster was steamed, smoothed dry to fit every part of the frame, cylinder, and barrel of the Colt inside. Finally, every outline of the gun could be seen on the front of the holster. When finished, the gun rode ever so lightly in its handfitted home. When palmed, the Colt slid from leather with no resistance. Once the hammer thong was slipped off and the tie-down in place, the gun simply waited its master's command.

Shannon had all he needed to back his play.

The hotel clerk, without undue pressure, told him the name of the storekeeper, Aaron Leiberman, but stubbornly refused to give information about the girl. He launched into an arrogant lecture on how strangers in town should mind their own business. As he warmed to the task his squeaky voice rose higher and higher. A veiled threat was issued, one personally insulting, "Mister, if you want to enjoy good health stop asking about the girl and your attackers. A lot of folks like you are so dumb they can't understand good advice."

Few things rankled Shannon more than people who assumed such self-importance. He could have conveniently said, "I really don't know," or "I rather not discuss this, if you don't mind," and that would have been the end of the matter. Shannon had been polite and soft-spoken. Instead he was berated by a pompous little jackass braying in his ear. Under his breath, Shannon said, "There's nothing more disgusting in this world than a little man in a little job."

Shannon entered Leiberman's store with reluctant steps, thinking, *Perhaps I should go back and apologize to the hotel clerk. After all it was something of an insult to hit a man with an open backhand rather than a closed fist. That blow had been a little stronger than intended. Maybe when he came to, he would be a bit more polite.*

Within minutes the conversation between Leiberman and Shannon was as friendly and open as that of two drifting cowhands by a campfire. The give and take of words had scarcely begun when Shannon could tell he had encountered a man of refinement and depth of character.

For the next hour or so, the story of what had occurred in Stillwater unfolded. The men who had done the dragging were the hands of a former Union colonel by the name of Hall. He had moved into the area from south Texas, driving about fifteen hundred head of cattle. Rumor had it they were of mixed brands. The ranch was located about fifteen miles south of town and claim was staked on some two hundred thousand acres. With him were ten or twelve hard-bitten riders—surly, aggressive, and mean. Hall seemed to have unlimited capital and quickly made the town largely dependent upon him financially. From all outward appearances Hall was a gentleman, who spoke with a clipped British accent.

Trouble had begun, however, as soon as the outfit settled in. The Hanks's ranch and the Dobbs's ranch, which bordered the colonel's were soon absorbed into Hall's so-called holdings. Dobbs's was found bushwhacked. He was shot in the back and again in the head at close range.

A few weeks later Hanks pulled out. Two of his hands had died in a line shack fire. The walls had been riddled with bullets and the smell of coal oil had hung heavy in the air. The following week rustlers made off with his small herd. Less than a month later Hanks sold out to Hall for a mere pittance. Suspicion centered on Hall but nothing could be proved. Stillwater had no sheriff or marshal. The nearest court was well over a hundred miles away. The entire matter was dropped.

Leiberman then shared with Shannon the information he earnestly wanted, the names of those who had accosted him in the street, and knowledge of the girl.

Those who hassled him were a couple of Slash L riders, Rinker and Pach. They had come into the country with Hall. Rinker was a gunman of some reputation but favored killing from ambush. Pach was part Apache, pure renegade.

The woman, however, was a different story. The colonel—ostensibly for the good of the children of the town, but actually to gain popularity—had built the schoolhouse and sent away for a teacher.

A few months later the new schoolmarm, Rachel Southerland, arrived. She was of such striking beauty the colonel laid claim to her immediately, without her consent or encouragement. Tragically she had signed a binding contract to teach for three years.

Within the first year Rachel began to win the respect and admiration of the townsfolk. After school she assisted Doc Blanchard whenever there was a medical emergency. She had learned basic nursing skills working in hospital wards to help pay finishing school expenses. In fact, she had been offered full time employment at the hospital after graduation but had turned it down to accept the teaching post in Stillwater.

Her motto "It is no sin to be ignorant, remaining so is the sin" soon caught on with the children and the adults of Stillwater. She was a demanding but fair and loving taskmaster. Within two years she had won the day for education.

To speak against Miss Rachel, or commit any act which would harm her, would call the entire community to her defense. That's why the townsfolk and those of the outlying farms and ranches were so concerned about Hall's overt possessiveness.

She had been reared in a respectable St. Louis family whose mother had inherited wealth. Her father was a poor businessman and an even poorer gambler. He rapidly squandered his wife's inheritance. By the age of ten, Rachel's family was impoverished, her father a victim of suicide and her mother a recluse. While Rachel was working her way through finishing school, her brothers and sisters married. The year she finished her mother was institutionalized. She felt the opportunity to teach in Stillwater at a salary of four hundred dollars a year was a godsend. Upon arriving in Stillwater she found herself in a most delicate situation. Hall was courteous and considerate, but let it be known that she had been spoken for. She had turned back his every advance but the situation was becoming dangerous. Hall was becoming more and more obsessive.

"Let me put it to you this way," said Leiberman. "Anyone, no matter who, that makes an overture, even the slightest, to Miss Rachel is discouraged rather forcefully by the colonel."

"Do you mean to tell me that he attempts to keep any possible suitor at bay with the idea that by isolating Rachel she will eventually accept him?" Shannon asked.

"That's exactly what I mean. It was he who gave Rinker and Pach orders to attack you. He was standing just inside the door of the saloon at the back of the group you saw," Leiberman added.

"Has this happened before?" Shannon asked.

"It's a regular occurrence here in Stillwater," Leiberman replied. "Every drummer, traveling cowpoke, and ranch hand that hits town can't help but admire Miss Rachel. In fact, you can bet if the colonel knew I was talking with you about this, he would try to have my store boycotted."

The forthright honesty of Leiberman impressed Shannon. His hand was automatically extended to him as an act of friendship and appreciation. Leiberman watched as Shannon's face took on a resolute appearance.

In emotionally charged words Shannon said to Leiberman, "I'm starting a ranching operation some thirty to forty miles from of here. Hopefully, it will become a large spread in just a few years. You'll have my business. Now, I tell you this. I don't hold with breaking the laws of God or man, but no one is going to stop me from exercising my legal rights and personal freedoms. The minute I saw Rachel I began falling in love with her. Someday I will marry her if she will have me. That, however, will be her decision. I'll also build that ranch. I have filed on every inch of the land, and I have a treaty with the Northern Cheyenne to graze cattle on land that is theirs by right of conquest in exchange for beef when their village needs food. Now that I have had my say, I'll go call on Pach and Rinker."

Leiberman walked to the back of the store where a clerk stood stocking the shelves, and said, "Andy, that's a fine young fellow, but he's swinging too wide a loop. If he braces Pach and Rinker at the same time, there'll probably be another fresh grave tomorrow." Leiberman would know quickly that Shannon was not a man to underestimate.

Stepping to the door of the saloon Shannon closed his eyes for a moment and opened them only a slit as he eased through the swinging door. They adjusted quickly to the dim interior of the room whose only light was that coming through the door and a couple of dirty side windows. Oil lamps hanging from the ceiling were never lit until after sundown due to the cost of coal oil.

Pach and Rinker sat at a table, a half-finished bottle before them. Rinker looked up, saying, "Well, if it ain't the rope slider all prettied up and ready to leave town." Pach added his two cents worth, saying, "Let's see if'en we can't show him the way to Mexico or the undertaker. Don't make no difference to me. The boss plumb despises men who make advances toward his intended."

To contain the inner rage was impossible. Shannon barked, "On your feet, you two miserable excuses for human beings. I'm going to read to you just like I did to Norton from the gospel of Colt, chapter 44, verse 40. You Slash L boys are too hard headed. Perhaps Norton didn't warn you, but he should have."

With a snarl Pach leapt to his feet, hand flashing for his gun. A totally shocked expression masked his face as his hand rose upward from holster to throat. He tried to speak. Only a gurgling sound rose to his lips as he fell across the table. Protruding from his neck was the steel handle of a knife.

Rinker rose ever so slowly to his feet, then became rigid.

"Don't even think about it, Rinker. If you so much as blink an eye or twitch a finger, I'll kill you," Shannon warned.

Rinker read in the eyes of the man before him a death notice. His words were as cold as the marble of a tombstone. Rinker had taken part in many a gun battle. Actually, he had never feared to face any man head on, but this was different from anything he had ever experienced—Pach killed in a split second, never clearing leather. Killed with a knife thrown so quickly, he scarcely saw the movement. Inside, Rinker turned to jelly. He did not know this man who confronted him. One thing he did know: He would either walk out of the saloon headed for parts unknown or be carried out dead and on the way to boot hill. He slowly unbuckled his gun belt and let it drop to the floor. "Before I leave, if you let me, tell me who you are," Rinker managed to asked.

"My name is Shannon. If I ever lay eyes on you again this side of heaven or hell, I'll drop you on the spot," Shannon sternly warned him.

At the name "Shannon," Rinker's knees weakened. It was a name whispered in awe among the best of gunmen—Shannon of the blinding fast draw and uncanny accuracy. His gun skill was legendary and he was known to be equally as fast with a knife. No one seemed to know how many had died bracing him. Those who knew, however, truthfully took the position they'd rather goose a grizzly with a toothache than face Shannon's gun, knife, or fist.

The room was as silent as the setting of the sun. A spider could have been heard walking across the ceiling. Shannon's piercing eyes scanned the room, looking into the face of every man in the place. There were several others present who had stood by during the dragging. They had been in the group on the saloon porch.

"Rinker, before you or anyone else leaves this room, someone is going to tell me the name of the man who ordered my dragging," Shannon said. To the last man they realized Shannon would broach no reluctance on their part to give him the information he wanted. He would get his answer or others would incur his wrath.

Nothing plagued Shannon's soul like the smug superiority some people possessed. Those who made right relative to money, or power, or social position, or political influence.

In Eastern towns and villages social orders were almost ironclad and people learned them imperceptibly by daily life. In every community there were those who could say whatever they wanted to say, do whatever they elected to do. They were always right in statement and act, no matter how ethically wrong they were. How much they hurt others was of little or no concern.

In North and South every person had a place, a sphere of existence from which it was difficult to move. Each individual was neatly pigeonholed. In the North there were specific niches for the Irish, Italian, German, Pole, and French. In the South there were the white and white trash, plantation owner and slave, aristocrat and commoner. From one end of the East to the other all things were relative to who you were, what you were, where you came from, and the color of your skin.

The West was a different matter. It was the leveler of men. No man stood higher than another except by consent of the common man. Courage, integrity, honesty, forthrightness, diligence, and industriousness not race, color, or creed determined a man's place and value in the order of things.

Shannon said, "Understand me. There is a person among you who feels he can lord it over all other people in this town. He thinks he can play God determining their destiny. He seeks to do it with money and hired guns. He now knows my name. His I want."

No one spoke a word. The silence only increased the furies within Shannon, his eyes blazed. "Somebody here is going to tell me who that son of a she fox is. Then, I will have a come-to-Jesus meeting with him," Shannon added.

Out of the corner of his eye, Shannon saw movement. The bartender was swinging a short club. Response was instantaneous. Shannon's left hand shot out, grabbed him by the vest and shirtfront, lifting him off his feet and over the bar.

He had wrestled with the best in Cherokee and Cheyenne camps; fought in rings and on boat decks, pounded spikes, lifted ties and rails. In the mines and on right-of-ways his hands had become hardened and callused from swinging the single and double jack, loading and pushing carts of ore. He had wrestled steers, rocks, barrels of rail spikes, and whiskey. Shannon may not have been too long on years, but more than long enough in experience. At six-four with broad shoulders and bulging biceps, Shannon was two hundred and forty pounds of solid man from top to bottom.

The bartender, bullet headed and big as an ox, came off the floor with a roar. He dropped into a classic boxing stance and shuffled in on Shannon. He faked with a left and crossed with a whistling right. Skyrockets went off in Shannon's head as the fist connected solidly.

The man could fight, but was out of shape. Doubtless he had won many a rough-and-tumble contest with brute strength and rudimentary boxing skills. His style was to crowd, clinch, and grapple. Shannon's head cleared. As the bartender tried to push Shannon against the bar, Shannon ripped a driving left, then a right, to his soft belly. His fists seemed to sink in up to the wrist. It stopped him gasping, dead in his tracks. Before he could recover Shannon swung him around by the shoulder and went to work. It was no time to hold back. After all, Shannon thought he tried to brain me with that short club.

The bartender's chin dropped, and Shannon's left uppercut followed by a straight right glazed his eyes. He stepped back. It was all coming back to

Shannon. The hours of training, sparring with "The Mick" when he worked for the railroad the year before his first trail drive.

Shannon had learned well at the instruction of O'Rouark, at the time a mail clerk on the railroad. In his younger days he had been a contender, one of the great Irish fighters dubbed "The Mick" by all.

When O'Rouark first shook Shannon's hand, he turned it over and looked at his knuckles. The clinched fist was virtually flat with broad knuckles, almost five inches broad and six inches long.

"Glory be," Mick exclaimed, "a born boxer's hands. May the saints protect him upon whose body these shillelagh knots land." From that day on, as long as Shannon was with the rail crew, every evening was spent in learning from the Mick the real art of boxing.

Shannon's blows had slowed the bartender, but he was not down-and-out. He shook his head, lowered his shoulders and bored in. Rolling, Shannon slipped a left off his shoulder, but a right caught him flush. Shannon's knees sagged. The bartender reached out and grabbed a fist full of shirt, jerking Shannon toward him. His bullet head came toward Shannon like a battering ram. There was no way he could avoid the impact. The next thing Shannon knew, thick arms circled his body. He was straining to break Shannon's back.

For a moment, Shannon panicked; then the battle lust arose. It was time to put an end to such foolishness. There was more than one kind of hand-to-hand combat, and Shannon had become, over the years, familiar with several. Lifting his arms high, he chopped down, full force, with a slashing blow. The heels of his hands slammed into either side of the bartender's neck. The force of the blow virtually paralyzed him. His arms dropped as if lifeless.

Propping him against the bar Shannon spun him along it to the very end with rights thrown stiffly from rolling shoulders, the full weight of his body behind each blow.

When he slumped to the floor, Shannon straightened up, took a couple of deep breaths before turning to speak to the onlookers, and said, "Now, somebody tell me, who ordered me dragged?"

He must have looked demented because the saloon emptied as fast as a house of ill repute when a preacher walked in.

The only person left was the swamper, standing in the corner, mop in hand. When he spoke, it was barely more than a whisper. "It was Colonel Hall, owner of the Slash L that had you dragged," he said. "Since his wife died, he's fancied Miss Rachel. He wants to marry her, but she don't cotton to him. Anybody who pays court to her is asking for trouble. Fact is, I'll be in trouble for telling you this if anybody finds out. Too long he's run roughshod over this country!"

Shannon was surprised by the man. He was not the ordinary alcoholic bar sweep. His speech was slightly slurred but his voice hinted of cultured background, perhaps even professional training. Behind that façade of an emaciated alcoholic face were fleeting reminiscences of aristocracy.

This could be seen all over the West. Some came west to make tracks, others to cover tracks, and many to become trackless, escaping from the haunting specter of the yesteryear.

Shannon offered him his thanks and left the saloon, thinking when the ranch would be fully established and running, his helping hand would be extended to that man.

It was not the time to launch an all-out war against the colonel and his group of hard cases. There was a ranch to be established. In the order of things, that came first. If there was to be a no-holds-barred, winner-take-all fight between the Bar J and the Slash L, it had to be later. The Bar J simply was not ready. It would be months before the growing herd was settled in and all the ranch buildings were completed. Additional water holes were to be located and cleaned; coffer dams strengthened to handle spring thaws and early summer rains. Every line shack had to be provisioned; winter grazing areas among the protected valleys spotted; defensive positions situated and stocked with emergency ammunition and provisions; and the larders of the ranch made sufficient for a siege.

Deep inside, Shannon was convinced it would eventually come to all-out conflict between the Slash L and the Bar J. A nagging, disquieting feeling came over him whenever he thought of the colonel and some of his men. He felt their lives had connected previously in some tangible way, but when, he could not determine. It was almost as if some twisted circumstance or ironic fate was bringing them together in an inevitable bloody strife.

Weeks slipped past like so much sand trickling through one's fingers. A herd trailing from Texas over the Bozeman Trail arrived to be mixed with the Herefords already on the rich grass. Calves born on the drive were branded along with any other mixed, abandoned stock known as mavericks, which attached themselves to the herd.

The summer passed swiftly and the colors of autumn arrived. Haying meadows had been shorn of their lush sward. Some were ricked while the greater part was stored in makeshift pole sheds at convenient locations on nearby range.

Illinois was a natural-born farmer. There was a bumper grain crop and a cellar full of potatoes, onions, pumpkins, and squash. The beams of the lower part of the hay barn hung heavy with sacks of dried beans, stalks of drying peppers, strings of "leather britches"* and bunches of herbs. Between the Coops and Illinois, the prospect of a full winter's table was assured.

As often as possible, trips were made to town. Once there, Shannon and his men carefully avoided contact with Slash L riders. By picking and choosing those times of heaviest work on the ranches, it was possible to occasionally pay a visit to Rachel and to Leiberman. Bar J's crew would just smile a tolerant smile whenever Shannon remarked, "Guess I ought to go to town and pick up a few things." They all knew it translated into "I've gone as long as I can without seeing Rachel."

As time passed the relationship between Shannon and Rachel grew steadily more intense. Grat, Haskett, and Funk were forever chiding Shannon, accusing him of not only foot dragging but plain lack of courage to declare his intentions and marrying Rachel.

One night he confessed to Grat, "I can face a mossy back longhorn bull mean as a son of Satan without a quaver, but when I think of asking Rachel to marry me, I turn to putty. I know why. I can face death without fear, but stand in mortal dread of having Rachel reject me. If she said no, then it would be over." Shannon knew the depth of his love for Rachel. To him it was as wide as a Kansas sky and as great and as solid as the massive peaks of the Rockies. Rachel had never declared her love for him, yet he knew she deeply cared. Should she decline his proposal he would live the rest of his life enduring an inward sorrow that might turn his dreams to dust.

On several occasions Shannon's pa had said real love could not be expressed in words. For the first time in his life Shannon knew what was being felt in those rare moments when his pa looked at his ma or his ma looked at his pa in that certain way. The feelings expressed in those exchanges could not be contained in words.

Sooner or later Shannon knew it would happen, and it did. It was early evening. He and Rachel were standing by the door of the schoolhouse deep in conversation, oblivious of their surroundings when the colonel and several of his men rode up.

---

*   Green beans tied in long strings, blanched and hung out to be air-dried. When dried they had the appearance of leather britches.

Hall was livid with anger, saying, "You were warned about forcing yourself on Rachel! Now by God, I'll run you out of this country!"

Shannon's reply was curt. "Colonel, no one is running me anywhere. As for forcing myself on Rachel, let her speak for herself." He wanted desperately to say, "Rachel will you marry me?" Yet Shannon could not bring himself to speak the words. If he did, the unanswered question would hang over his head like the Sword of Damocles. It would be a moment of truth. Fulfillment of his dreams would depend upon a tiny word composed of three letters. *Yes. What would Rachel's reply be? Would it be, "Oh, yes, Shannon, I will," or a crushing reply of rejection such as, "Shannon, I wish I could but I just can't."* The thoughts running through Shannon's mind were halted by the colonel's reaction.

Hall flew into a jealous rage. From his lips poured a torrent of threats ending with, "This courting of Rachel will stop. It will stop now. Rachel is to be my wife. No other man will ever have her." As he continued, a maniacal demented force contorted his features, and every person present knew that Hall walked a fine line between sanity and madness. Only then did Shannon realize the colonel was a much older man than he thought. He had taken on the look of an aged grizzly filled with contempt and hatred for all humans.

Hall's men looked at each other with questioning eyes. At times his unreasoning temper and fitful moods had been witnessed by them, but nothing so erratic as this. For a moment he appeared to have turned into a different person. The last words he spoke as he wheeled his horse to ride away with bloody spurs raking its sides were "In good time, I'll finish the job started years ago, Shannon!"

Again, the unknown gripped Shannon. That vague, unsettling feeling came over him again. Was he a pawn in the hands of a capricious fate being irresistibly drawn to some watershed in his life? "A job started years ago," what did Hall mean? There was that other unanswered question, and Shannon knew it had to be resolved without any delay.

He took Rachel's hand and said, "Rachel, Hall said no man other than he would marry you. I don't believe that. You know my love for you. Can you find it in your heart to marry me." Rachel's answer, "Oh, yes, Shannon, I will," was instantaneous, but to him it seemed a lifetime coming.

The ugly confrontation with Hall faded but was not forgotten. Rachel had said yes. She had never seen the ranch. It was time for celebration and joy. The very next day they would go to the ranch and make all of their plans for the future.

Across the land autumn days were being caressed by the artistic hands of Mother Nature. Bank upon bank of fleecy clouds lazily nudged one another across a silky sky of bottomless blue. A bright sun skipped from cloud to cloud, painting the landscape with light and dark shadows. Slightly yellowing grass, with tall heads swaying in the breeze, were giving a farewell nod to summer and beckoning to a waiting winter.

As the two rode side by side there was almost a sacramental silence. Rachel and Shannon communicated with each other in glances of unconcealed emotion. Not a word broke the spell, as there flowed between them an intensity of feelings springing from the very depths of their inner beings.

Only one experience in life had prepared Shannon for such profound and mystifying communication. The deaths of his ma and pa had plunged him into the depths of bereavement with a puzzling result. Once he had passed through the shock of their deaths, and the days had lengthened into years, his parents seemed closer to him. There were even those times when he sensed their presence and heard their voices in the inner ear of his mind. Such moments were cherished, for they filled him with happiness and inexplicable joy. They were dead, yet in a real sense they lived and communicated with him in some unexplainable way.

Between Rachel and Shannon there was a sense of felt oneness, of mutual fulfillment, of combined destiny—not to mention sensitivity to each other's moods and emotional needs.

As they topped the rise, before them was a panoramic view of the far blue valley stretching for miles. Some would call it a hanging valley, since it seemed to be suspended between heaven and earth. At the near end, some two to three miles below, were the ranch buildings nestled on a shaded shelf. The two bold streams rushing from the heights above sparkled in the sunlight as they danced their way across the valley floor.

Shannon heard Rachel's sudden intake of breath. There was a startled gasp as she gazed for the first time at what would be her valley home. The stuff that dreams were made of sprung to life before her eyes.

Easing from the saddle, Rachel slipped to the ground. As they stood hand in hand, she spoke for the first time. "I don't think I ever want to leave this place."

"The good Lord willing you never will." Shannon's reply was filled with the future's hopes, but he did not know how prophetically true Rachel's words would be.

Rachel turned and leaned against Shannon. His arms slipped around her waist. He felt the softness of her lips as her body, filled with the promise of exquisite joys yet to come, melted against his.

For no reason other than that of sheer exhilaration, love, and celebration of happiness, they began to chase each other like children in a schoolyard, playing tag until they fell, laughing into a mass of tangled arms and legs.

Lying on the sun-drenched grass Shannon looked at Rachel with a fierce tenderness that could not be expressed in words. She trembled as he gently cupped her face in his hands and lightly brushed his lips across hers. For them there was no reserve, no blocking the mountainous wave of emotion. The moment of giving had come and every fiber of Shannon's being held Rachel in awesome wonder.

A wave of fresh understanding rushed to Shannon's mind. Rachel was totally vulnerable, baring her very being as a woman, willing upon the altar of love to give her most precious intimate self wholly, completely, and willingly to the man she loved. He was stunned by the thought of the responsibility that such unrestricted surrender placed upon him. The fierce driving male passion within to satisfy his burning urgent need was transformed into a no-less intense desire to give rather than take, to place her needs before his, to bind her to him in a passion which honored her giving and his receiving. In that moment heaven and earth passed away and the Garden of Eden was reborn. In each other's arms they slept the sleep of innocents.

Shannon was aroused by the sound of rushing feet. A murderous barrage of blows blotted out Rachel's screams. Again and again he struggled to come out of an abyss of ever-increasing pain as gun butts, boot heels, and toes hammered at his body and shredded the flesh of his chest and back. Each time the darkness was pushed back by sheer determination another wave of pain would bring a swirling vortex of unconsciousness and helplessness. In the rare moments of consciousness he heard Rachel's pitiable cries. Then deep unconsciousness, no matter how hard he fought against it, surged over him.

Brightness of a noonday sun warmed his body. Shannon lifted his head and tried to crawl on all fours, but convulsions of pain and racking nausea drove him back to the ground. He fainted again and was out for a time. Sometime later, how long he did not know, he finally stood up. Looking about, fearing what he might or might not see, he saw the worst. A few feet away was Rachel's lifeless, ravaged, and broken body.

Falling to his knees beside her the nightmare events began to flashback. It was all too real, too clear: the voices, the raucous laughter, the wanton words, the pleas of Rachel, her screams, snatches of conversation—"Colonel said . . ." "Do with her what you wish . . ." "Kill him . . ." "Make sure she's dead."

Only nature bore witness to the following soul struggle. Shannon stood rigidly erect, arms lifted to the skies. His head was matted with blood where the shot had plowed a gash across his head. His face blackened with powder burns from the muzzle blast. No wonder they thought him dead. From his throat there issued a primordial cry of anguish. It was similar to the bone-chilling wail of a panther in death throes or the scream of a horse trapped in a fire. No sound of high ridge or deep forest created such instant shock to the hearer.

Shannon turned his head to the north and from the depths of his tormented soul there arose his mother's chants to the Norse gods. His voice grew stronger and stronger. From a whisper to a cry, from a cry to a shout, "Odin, Odin, Odin." The valley below rang with his words as they fell from his lips. No human heard to answer. The spirits responded. Visions came, Vikings riding upon ships of clouds, brandishing their bloodied weapons of war. They swirled about Shannon's head and upon him poured out their battle lust.

The vision swiftly passed. He was snapped back to reality. With tender trembling hands he wrapped Rachel's body in a duster from his saddlebags. Holding her in his arms he climbed into the saddle and slowly rode to the ranch.

The crew gathered around him as he stopped at the fencing wagon and placed her body on its rough plank floor. Folding back the duster he took water from the keg lashed to the wagon and with a bandanna gently washed her face. Not one of the crew spoke a word. They had seen. They could read sign. It was enough.

Leading the horse, already harnessed to the wagon, Shannon slowly led a small procession to a knoll behind the ranch house. Taking pick and shovel from the wagon he dug the grave. Several of the men stepped up to help but one glance from him turned them back. He and he alone, would lay Rachel to rest.

By the time the grave was covered the entire ranch crew, even those who had been out on the range, had gathered on the knoll. No explanations were given. In fact, none were necessary. Their reaction was the same as that reflected in Shannon's eyes, but not with the same intensity.

Walking through the ranch house Shannon took from the gun cabinet a brand new Colt .44/40, checked the mechanism, filled the chambers, and dropped it in his holster. Another was stuck in his waistband. Within minutes he was in the saddle, headed for Stillwater.

Al Grat spoke up, saying, "The boss has a head start on us, and I don't know about you, but I'm not going to sit here and let the boss get shot up." To the last man they saddled up and headed for town armed to the teeth.

Stillwater was too quiet. An uneasy calm had settled over its streets. The only horses at the hitching rails carried the Slash L brand. Although it was early evening; all stores were closed, the stable deserted, and the most popular café without customers. There was no doubt the colonel's men expected riders from the Bar J bent upon revenge for killing of what they thought was both Rachel and Shannon. Across the street from the saloon other Slash L horses were lined up at the rail. The whole setup spelled trouble, a trap to eliminate as many of the Bar J as possible. *So be it*, Shannon thought. They would not be expecting him, and by all that was holy, he wouldn't disappoint them.

There was no fear of dying within Shannon, only the grim determination to take as many as possible of those who had killed Rachel to the grave with him. Nothing else mattered. It's difficult to threaten a man who doesn't care whether he lives or dies. In fact, at the moment, death seemed far more attractive to Shannon than life.

Shannon ghosted through the back door of the saloon. There were six Slash L riders inside, celebrating. Two of the six had livid scratches on their faces, probably from Rachel's fingernails. One chanced to look up. When he saw Shannon standing at the end of the bar, it so startled him he tipped his chair backward and fell against the wall. The other five looked up and saw what no guilty man ever wanted to see. Before them was judge, jury, and executioner in the form of an apparition from the bowels of hell.

Shannon was covered with blood and dirt; shirt hanging in shreds, pants ripped. The only thing about him that looked untouched were the guns. When he spoke, not one of them moved a muscle.

There was an almost demented look in his eyes. "She never harmed a one of you. She spoke to you with respect. Yet you destroyed her. Ravaged her body and killed her spirit with heartless lust. You are nothing more than loco rabid wolves. I buried her. Now I'm going to bury you. Take your shriveled souls and meet your maker," Shannon muttered.

As they went for their guns the few shocked onlookers in the saloon hit the floor. The abuse of a woman would not be tolerated in the West, especially one so well liked by so many as Rachel. If what Shannon stated was true, and there was no reason to doubt his word, then if he didn't settle the matter, the townsfolk would with rope and stable beam.

One witness, who said he was staring directly at Shannon, later described what he saw.

"Those not in the know can't believe what I saw. Shannon's gun just materialized in his hand and spouted flame. Red was slammed against the wall a widening splotch of blood on his shirt pocket. Dover's gun was just beginning to clear leather when two shots erupted like rolling thunder. He was twisted around and fell across a table, gun half in his holster. Then it was all sound and fury, crashing volleys of gunfire from door and window. The bartender stupidly joined Slash L's play. His body was slumped over the bar, an unfired shotgun in hand. Seven men put down in only a few seconds of gunplay! If I didn't know it then, I know it now. The Bar J outfit is a bunch of curly wolves. There were as devil-may-care as a feisty young puppy chasing a cougar through hell. There just weren't no stopping them. The colonel has bit off more than he can chew this time. If he does and tries to swallow, he'll choke to death."

The action brought Shannon back from a trancelike state. Scattered about on the floor were the bodies of six Slash L riders and that of the bartender across the bar. Going into the street an equally grim sight was found. Haskett, Grat, and Funk had pussyfooted into town from the north, leaving their mounts the other side of the bridge. The Coops, Hatton twins, Ruble, and Illinois had slipped in from the south end of town. They, like Shannon, had anticipated an ambush. With pistols and Greener double barrel shotguns they had cleared the snakes out of their holes. All in all the Slash L lost ten men. One had survived with minor wounds. He was a pitiful sight.

Outside Funk and Ruble stood, flanking the sole surviving Slash L rider in town. The hangman's noose was around his neck. Ruble held the coiled rope in one hand. A grim-faced Funk turned to Shannon, saying, "Boss, we waited for you to do the honors," Some of the Bar J hands, along with a group of the townspeople, had gathered in front of the livery. Above the upper story of the stable protruded a beam with block and tackle. Someone had shimmied up the rope and let the tackle down. Another had driven a buckboard in place. A justifiable hanging was in offing.

"Big Coop, you and Haskett take the rope off that man. I need a messenger boy," Shannon ordered. "He ain't nothing but a pie-faced kid anyway, who fancies himself a gun hand." Shannon's words of reprieve ended the kid's begging to live.

"Ride to the colonel. Tell him what has happened here. Let him know I am alive and well, and that I don't yet know why he has such hatred for me. When I do figure it out, however, we'll have a conversation he'll never forget," Shannon said.

"I'll tell him every word you have said. I surely will. Can I leave now?" the kid begged.

"Hold your horses, boy. There's a bit more to tell the colonel. This you brand in your memory, word for word. Better still, someone get me pencil and paper. I'll write it down," Shannon said. Once finished, Shannon handed the note to him and ordered, "Now ride! If you don't deliver this message to the colonel, I'll come after you with this rope. The next time you'll be swinging in the breeze."

Everyone in the crowd wondered what Shannon had written. It was a simple statement meant to irk the colonel: "Men do not make the West, the West makes men. Think on this until we meet."

CHAPTER 8

Range War

Had Shannon not been obsessed with overcoming his grief by retaliation, numbing his pain by pouring out white hot lead, he would have sensed the unreasonableness of his hasty action. Rachel's death had caused Shannon to react on the basis of emotion alone. A driving desire to taste the bittersweet fruits of revenge led to a tragic oversight, not only on his part but the rest of the ranch crew. To the man, they had miscalculated the cunning strategy of their enemy. Upon arrival at the ranch from Stillwater, it was found to be in shambles. Hall had struck hard. When less than one third of Hall's gunhands were found in Stillwater, Shannon should have reasoned the remainder had been held back for an assault on the ranch.

Evidently the colonel suspected the hands would react as they did. Even as they left the ranch for the showdown in town, a group of his forces were in the high tops overlooking the ranch. When the Bar J crew left the ranch, the Slash L riders rode in, pillaging, burning, and wrecking everything in sight. Barn and stable where charred ruins. Corrals were pulled down and emptied of stock. The main house and the bunkhouse, built mostly of stone with heavy beams sustained the least damage. They could be made inhabitable again within a short time, but it would take days to round up the horses and discover what had happened to the cattle. Were the cattle simply scattered or rustled?

This was the colonel's way of breaking the spread. Three things he had not figured on, but most of all that Shannon was not killed with Rachel.

The first was the reaction of the men of Bar J. The colonel did not know it was actually their ranch as well as Shannon's. He had stirred up a hornet's nest. Hall did not understand that men bound together by a common golden dream, men certain they are in the right, never give up. He had attacked the brand for which they rode and in which they had a vested interest. They were proud of the Bar J and would die for it. They were as loyal to the brand as they had been to the flags under which several of them had served during the war. They were willing to risk their lives for their way of life.

Secondly, the colonel had not reckoned with the reaction of the people of Stillwater as the story of what happened to Rachel spread among the townsfolk. For the first time they acceded to his demands but did so with reluctance and lack of civility. His hands were tolerated, nothing more. There was talk of vigilantes and lynching, but cooler heads prevailed. Shannon let it be known that he would settle the matter once and for all.

In the last instance the colonel had no way of knowing Shannon's fortunate monetary reserves. Word had come from Louisville as to his profits from the keelboat and freighting ventures. There were ample funds to rebuild and restock the ranch. Restocking, with a newly purchased herd, would not break him.

Shannon, as well as the crew, reasoned the herd had been scattered. They were all branded stock. Hall wouldn't dare rustle and attempt to dispose of the herd anywhere within a hundred miles of Stillwater. If the cattle were still somewhere in the country, they could be found. To round them up would divide Shannon's forces and make it easier for Hall's hired killers to set up ambushes. The tactic of divide and conquer, as one of the most successful military tactics ever devised was being used by Hall with deadly results.

Stillwater was the only available source of needed supplies. Whether his men could get into town and back unnoticed with the goods was another matter. Nonetheless the chance had to be taken.

The caches were still intact. Supplies there, however, were planned to sustain a couple of men, four at the most, for a week. Only a hundred rounds of ammunition had been secreted in each cache. That was not nearly enough for an all-out range war with the Slash L, which could last for weeks, maybe months.

Food at the main ranch was in short supply. It would be half rations until provisions were obtained. What hurt most was the absence of coffee. A hot cup of Arbuckles, with an added pinch of chicory, was almighty comforting around a lonely camp at the shank end of a day of chasing and being chased. That was exactly what it would be until the conflict was over. Neither Slash L nor Bar J would rest until the last shot was fired.

This was no minor skirmish. The hostilities would not end until Hall or Shannon, perhaps both, were dead. The murder and rape of Rachel had ended any hope of a peaceful resolution. Shannon now had allies, the people of Stillwater, yet he did not want vigilante justice. It was his fight until the law was brought to Stillwater. Although the citizens of Stillwater were for the most part law-abiding folks, Shannon could not depend on them holding Hall to accountability. They had not previously stood against Hall. If he did not stop Hall, who had cowered the town once, then there was no reason to believe they would not again knuckle under to his designs.

Leiberman would have what was needed. With a bit of notice he would arrange to meet the wagons under the cover of night. Even that would be risky. It would be best if purchases could be made during normal business hours which would attract less attention. All of the Bar J were known men and the wagons easy to identify. The problem's answer came unexpectedly.

Lookouts posted on the ridges above access routes to the ranch flashed a warning with mirrors that three strangers were approaching the ranch from the direction of Stillwater. The men scattered to defensive positions leaving Big Coop, Haskett, and Shannon as a greeting party.

Three of the saltiest characters anyone would lay eyes on slowly pulled past the ruins of the barn and stable, then up to those standing in front of the burned-out ranch house. One rode while the other two drove heavy freight wagons, used by buffalo hunters. Their mounts were hitched behind. Resting by the seat of the lead driver were three Sharps rifles in fringed leather cases. This was a trio to be walked around softly. Their horses were typical cow ponies, well fed, groomed, wide of girth, and built for endurance. They all wore homespun shirts, black vests, and brown sailcloth Levi's. There was a Winchester in each saddle scabbard and snugged in their holsters were well-worn Colts. These were knowing and cautious riders. Although their hands were in sight the hammer thongs had been slipped from their six-guns.

"We'd be right proud to ride in if this is the Bar J outfit. If it ain't, we'd appreciate someone pointing out the way," one of the men said.

Haskett stepped out in plain sight from the corner of the ranch house, saying, "'Bout time you troublemakers showed up. Why, I sent for you weeks ago. What kept you?"

Coop and Shannon were astonished at the striking similarity between Haskett and the strangers. They appeared to all having been cut from the same bolt of cloth.

"Shannon, Coop, these are three of the orneriest, bowleggedest, lyingest grub line riders you ever saw. This here's three of my cousins from the Smokies: Jubal, Justus, and Jared."

Shannon with a nod of his head spoke, "Lite down and sit a spell. Any kin of Haskett's is more than welcome."

"They've been riding scout for the army when they won't feuding, generally hell-raising, or buffalo hunting. Heard they were just lying around Fort Bridger going to seed so I sent for them. Figured the way things were shaping up we might need help. Actually they come out of nothing more than sheer worship of my manly powers and good looks," Haskett said.

The four Hasketts set to jawing in language so colorful one could see it when they talked. They cussed each other more ways than a cowboy could spin a tall tale, all the while grinning like a mule eating briars.

When they finally let up to a slow gallop, Shannon butted in, "We're going to be in the middle of an all-out shooting war here shortly. I don't want you caught in the middle. Such as we've got, you're welcome to, but it might be wise to ride on. Ordinarily we would feed you, snug you in, and sing you to sleep."

Jubal with a characteristic mountain drawl, spoke up in reply to Shannon, "Cousin Haskett, this fellow is a might heavy on words and slight on understanding. Why back home there won't nothing we'd rather do than fight less it was walking out after night preaching with one of those saucy Goins girls. Cousin informed us you might have a snake or two that needed skinning. Why we'd take it right unneighborly if you deprived us of delivering into the hands of the almighty a raw sinner or two."

Big Coop let out a deep chuckle, "Boss, set 'em to the table. Back during my army days the major said these three Hasketts could whip a squad when sober and annihilate more than a company when drunk."

The crew was increased by three and a major problem was solved. Early the next morning the three left for Stillwater. Their wagons had been unloaded and fresh horses hitched up. Unknown to the Slash L town informers, they could obtain what was needed from Leiberman's store without becoming suspect. Once resupplied, plans could be made for the battle ahead. When the Hasketts returned, the ranch site would be temporarily abandoned, and the crew split up to scour the country for the scattered herd. Once found they would be driven to safety in one of the high mountain valleys. With the herd secured, a base camp from which to attack the Slash L would be set up.

For two weeks, from breaking dawn to gathering night, the round up occupied every waking moment. Finally the remnants of the original herd were bedded down in a blind high valley concealed by rising peaks on three sides. There was ample water and the floor of the valley was deep with drying grass.

Fall and winter were rapidly approaching and the showdown had to come before the onset of harsh weather. It was imperative that the ranch be made once again livable, and the herd brought down from the heights to warmer valleys below. In the high country, winter's frozen fist often became an unyielding force destroying herds while making life utterly miserable for every range rider. It could and did destroy men and animals.

Each knew the easy part was past. A range war would now stalk the wooded and rocky hills, lush valleys, streets of Stillwater, and lonely hidden trails. Men would die. Preachers or friends would say words over them. Graves would be filled. Life and dreams would be ended or assured.

It was business made nastier when the opponent was without honor, devoid of principle. Among the Bar J there was not one reluctant warrior. Each would give his opponent a fair chance in a shootout. Heaven help, however, the bushwhacker or ambusher for they would receive in turn precisely what they had given. Shannon and his riders would keep coming; relentless, implacable, and merciless until justice was done and individual rights restored.

The Slash L had made right relative to their hired guns, right relative to Hall's despotic whims, right relative to their financial control of the town, and right relative to their power and desires. Those whose rights are so denied will ultimately rise up and throw off the shackles of their oppressor. At times it was accomplished at the ballot box, on other occasions in the halls of justice. But in the West, when necessary, it was achieved by six-gun retribution.

All was quiet in the dusky dark as a rider approached the camp. The herd, being driven to its winter graze, had stopped milling and was settling down for the night. A slight stamping of hoofs and the pricked ears of the mustangs in the remuda had already announced his coming.

The Hasketts, all four of them rose silently to their feet, rifles in hand, and melted into the gathering of darkness. The twins moved to either side of the fire, and slightly to the front, with their backs to the glow. These two were no pilgrims. Their eyes quickly adjusted to the oncoming darkness. True, they were silhouetted by the fire, but they knew if any threatening move was made by the rider, Ruble would without hesitation empty his saddle.

"Hello, the camp. I'm Sanders looking for the Bar J," the rider said. In the quiet his voice carried well. Something about it caused both of the twins to ease off their hammer thongs. Big Coop, seeing their reaction, took three steps back, and slid his hand under a sack at the back of the chuck wagon, grasping the checkered stock of a Greener shotgun.

Dap issued the invitation, "Ride on in and set a spell." Sanders eased from the saddle. "I'm riding the grub line, looking for work. Near 'bout starved to death. Fellow, this side of Stillwater said you were making a gather. Hoped you'd need another hand," Sanders said.

Shannon, who had been listening in the darkness, stepped into the light and said, "I'm the ramrod of this outfit. We have a full crew, but you are welcome to camp fare: beans, fat back, and sourdough."

As Sanders filled his plate and cup, the boys began to drift in from the herd, leaving only the nightriders. Those who had heard what he said knew he was lying. No starving man could wolf down three plates of beans. A belly empty for a couple of days can't take that much food all of a sudden. Shannon suspected a set up. Who had sent him?

A partial answer came when Sanders pulled from his pocket a folded piece of paper, which he handed to Shannon. "Fella' back on the trail was heading this way to deliver a message. Asked me to give you this," said Sanders.

Unfolding the page and holding it low to the light of the fire it simply read, "Come as soon as possible. I need your help." It was signed "Lieberman." Shannon straightened up and threw a whistling right to Sanders' jaw. The impact sounded like that of a large flat rock dropped in mud.

"Lordy!" one of the Hasketts exclaimed, "You hit him so hard you probably killed half his family." Shannon turned, grimfaced to those gathered about the unconscious Sanders.

"The whole thing has to be a set up. Sanders wasn't starving. No man starved out stuffs his stomach," Shannon said. "Besides that, it's Leiberman's signature all right, but his name is spelled wrong. The Slash L is probably trying to lure us away from what's left of the herd. They may be planning to ambush us if we ride in, or even along the way. Hall knows we are indebted to Leiberman. He also knows I survived the attack when Rachel was killed and is determined to finish the job. Nonetheless, we have to go and check on Leiberman, no matter what the cost. He has stood by us. We'll stick by him. I believe somebody forced him to write this note."

A plan of action was quickly adopted. Funk, Ruble, Grat, and Shannon would approach the town first. Shannon, along with Grat would go to the saloon while Funk and Ruble worked their way through the alleys to cover the main drag. Six were sent out to ride night herd in case there was an attempt to rustle the cattle. Three would remain in camp with Greeners, which Shannon favored over Colt revolving shotguns.

The Colt was a powerful and deadly weapon but had been known to chain fire with flame leaping from one charged chamber to the next igniting the charges in rapid sequence. When this happened, the Colt could kill or maim on both ends.

Sanders was stripped of clothes and boots, carried three or four miles out and put afoot in his underwear. Shannon didn't want him hotfooting it back to town warning the Slash L of their plans.

Shannon cautioned the men, "If this is a trap, then as soon as the shooting stops, win, lose, or draw, scatter out to the line shacks and the caches, gather up the food and ammunition, and head for the rendezvous below Rockface. When braced we'll have to be heavy on lead and light on mercy."

Stillwater was not totally asleep as Shannon's crew slipped into town. The only light was that fanning out across the plank floor in front of the saloon and spilling into the street. Funk and Ruble had tied their mounts behind the blacksmith's shop. Removing their spurs, they silently moved up an alley to the main street directly in front of the saloon.

Shannon and Al shed their boots and slipped on moccasins taken from their saddlebags. They merged with the darkness and moved to the back of the saloon. Shannon whispered, "Al, Injun around to the front, I'll go in the back door. When I start my play, join in."

The knob turned noiselessly. Pushing ever so lightly, the door began to ease open. Then, as usual, the best-laid plans of men and the gods went haywire. Hinges, long unused and exposed to sun and rain, gave off a high-pitched squeak. There was no recourse but to slam open the door and face the music.

A Slash L rider standing inside the front door with gun in hand whirled, dropped into a crouch, and fired. Not only was he fast, but accurate. A halo of flame shone brightly around the muzzle of his gun. Searing pain came as the bullet ripped through flesh. The wound was not mortal but enough to make Shannon consider his mortality.

Shannon palmed his gun as an instant reflex. Two drumming shots erupted. The first staggered the gunhand. The second tumbled him into a lifeless heap on the floor. Al Grat stepped over the body and joined the party. It lasted but a few seconds. Acrid smoke filled the room. Two Slash L riders were sprawled, still in death, in the corner. Two others were cringing against the wall opposite the bar, hands widespread away from their guns. One had a shoulder wound, the other a spreading stain on his side. They had seen gunfights before but nothing had prepared for them the utter finality found in the guns of the Bar J.

Shannon's cold eyes turned on them as he warned, "There's horses at the rail. I suggest you head for one of the Cs, California or Canada. If I or any of my men see you again this side of the Pearly Gates, either heading up or down, we'll hang you."

They hit the door running and were met with a crashing volley of shots which ripped them to shreds. Slash L's rooftop ambushers, thinking they were Bar J riders, had cut them down. That was answered by a steady, probing, withering lethal fire from Funk and Ruble's Henry rifles.

An eerie silence hung over the street. There is no silence like that of a battlefield after the guns are muted. It lasted, however, but a moment.

The lead had burned its way from the front to the back of Shannon's side. A spreading stain on his shirt indicated an ugly gash had been cut deep in the flesh. Al got one through the meaty part of his thigh when the street hideouts had downed their own. All other Bar J riders had come through the fray somewhat unscathed. Bloodied, but far from beaten, Shannon and his men sprung to their saddles.

Had the Slash L hit their temporary camp or the ranch again in their absence was the question running through the mind of Shannon. Every man jack of the ambuscade in the saloon were guns for hire. Not top gunmen like Thompson, Short, Fisher, Settlemeyer, or Earp, but tough, fast gunhands who worked for the highest bidder. Men who lived by the creed of gain, their loyalty was not to the brand but to the payroll. Their outfits were above average. Their clothes a bit too new, neither work nor travel weary. Their pockets were often filled with blood money. That which occupied the greater part of their lives was gambling and drinking. Within their lives was a wasteland. They either liked you for a dollar or betrayed you for one. Such men died before the shrine to which they gave their allegiance—the dollar mark. They did not build for the future or enhance the present. They were takers rather than givers, and the world was well rid of them.

In the heat of battle Shannon had forgotten Leiberman's note. Was he actually at the store? Was he in imminent danger? Shannon wheeled his horse and headed for Leiberman's. Leaping from the saddle he burst through the door only to be met with a thundering blast out of the darkness. As he momentarily blacked out he thought to himself, *Somebody tripped me.* It seemed as if someone had caught his ankle not in an iron grip, but with a gentle touch, just enough to cause the fall. *Dear God,* Shannon whispered to himself, *It was here that I fell the first time I saw Rachel. Was it her gentle spirit which had now saved my life?* The blast of the shotgun had gone over his head. Had it not, he would have been graveyard dead. Rising from the floor Shannon heard someone running, and the back door of the store slamming shut. The assailant had escaped.

Muffled scuffing sounds came from the storeroom. Leiberman had been bound and gagged. When released, he told Shannon what had happened. As the shooting started, all the Slash L men had left the store except for one. It was midnight dark in the store but Leiberman recognized the man's voice.

"It was Hall, himself," Leiberman said. He ordered the men out, telling them that he, and he alone, would put Shannon down. It was a personal vendetta. He was the one behind the shotgun.

Outside there was a crashing of shots as additional Slash L men rode in to be met by the Bar J hands waiting for Shannon. There were too many Hall guns. Shannon's men knew their orders. Scatter to the four winds, hit the secret caches and line cabins for food and ammunition, and then regroup at a small hidden-valley cave at Rockface high up on Roughbutt. There they would wait for all the hands who were able to come in. No unnecessary moves would be made to leave trails for Hall's trackers.

Leiberman had taken Shannon's horse to the side alley by the store. Supplies had been placed in the saddlebags. His wounds were hastily dressed. Shannon had to move and move fast. Hall's men were all over the town. The wounds, shoulder and side, were alive with burning pain and badly bleeding; but he, with Leiberman's help, managed to get into the saddle and head for the mountains. After only a brief period of riding Shannon blacked out.

How long he had been riding he did not know. Steel gray skies tinged pink by an afternoon sun spread over the western horizon. It finally penetrated his foggy brain that he had been in the saddle since late the previous night. His mountain-bred mustang, which had more bottom than any horse he had ever owned, was barely moving. His head drooped and steps faltered. Shannon stroked the horse's neck with palsied hands, feeling the muscles rigid from exertion. Both man and mount were bone weary.

Above the peaks, rising from the unfamiliar valley below, were leaden skies. Rippling clouds piled into ever-thickening folds sent a message of imminent danger. Snow driven by a screaming northerner would soon blanket the landscape with a thick shroud of white.

Shannon, slumped in the saddle, urged his horse ahead, aware of the threat to both. His wounds had stopped bleeding. The loss of blood previously and the bitter cold, however, made the prospect of freezing to death all too real. His fatigue was matched by an increasing melancholy. He had to find shelter where he could build a fire, tend to his wounds, care for his horse, and prepare food.

Even though dead beaten, done in, and played out, Shannon scanned the valley below from the stand of heavy timber where he sat his horse. A vast emptiness stared back at him. There was little movement except for a buck and three does feeding quietly at the lower end of the meadow. Where the valley rose to meet the foot of the mountains there was a small herd of elk.

Starting within a hundred yards of the edge of the timber screen where he was located, Shannon glassed with his binoculars every swell, clump of bushes, or patch of berries in the valley. Each contour, every undulation, rock, fallen tree, and grass hump was examined with care. In unfamiliar territory such caution often meant the difference between life and death. He was alive and intended to stay that way until Hall was finally defeated. Satisfied that it was reasonably safe he began moving around the perimeter of the valley, well back from the grassy floor, hidden by a wall of trees.

Fueled by sheer determination, Shannon finally reached the other side of the valley and began following a faint trail. While glassing the rising heights, he had seen a dark spot, perhaps a rock overhang or a cave. It was to that landmark he was headed when the main trail gave out. Before him was little more than a game trail or a footpath. Higher and higher it rose becoming less distinct with each step. It had been unused for years.

Rounding a switchback, the mustang faltered and suddenly stopped. From a semidaze, Shannon was jerked into awareness. As his eyes focused, before him stood a cabin jutting from the rock. It had been built against an overhang with front and side logs chinked with mud mortar. The remainder of the stone shelter had been walled with piled stones, about six to seven feet high, creating a shelter for two or three mounts or pack animals. It was a mountain man's home, perhaps a hundred years old, yet still snug and in good repair.

Faint from weakness, and chilled to the bone, Shannon half fell from the saddle. The movement brought searing pain, which in itself was more of a blessing than a curse. It cleared his head, shocking him into alertness. Exhausted as he was, he had to care for his horse. Stripping the gear from the mustang, he rubbed him down with a half-rotten sack found in the stable. Staggering outside, he gathered half an armful of grass, tossed it into the shelter, and holding to the wall, finally managed to enter the cabin.

Opening the door of the heavy hand-hewn planks hung on rusty horseshoe hinges, he stepped inside and threw his saddlebags down by the hearth. A coat of dust like a gray blanket covered everything. There was wood by the fireplace. Nearby, a trough carrying spring water from outside ran crystal clear.

In moments Shannon had a fire going. Soon water was boiling, and the smell of coffee in the making filled the room. The dry wood made little smoke to reveal his presence, yet he had to chance it. He did not know what kind of tracks he had left behind. Semiconscious there was no way he could have covered his trail. If they looked, they would find him soon enough unless snow covered his tracks.

He had found the things so desperately needed in the saddlebags Leiberman had packed. There was coffee, dried beans, a cut of side meat, bit of salt, a small wedge of cheese, and a fist-size chunk of beef wrapped in sourdough. Scattered in the bottom of the bags was a double handful of .44/40s.

Sitting on the hearth, Shannon busied himself cleansing his wounds while drinking cup after cup of hot water with a pinch of salt in it. As a boy his pa told him how salt water was given to those who lost a lot of blood and how much good it had done. True or not, it was making him feel better.

Dragging himself upright, Shannon began to rummage about every nook and cranny of the room, hoping to find something with which he might treat his wounds. In one cabinet he found some remnants of cloth, musty but clean. The back corner of a cupboard yielded a bottle of turpentine, half evaporated. The remainder was dark and syrupy. When he finally uncorked the bottle, the pungent smell indicated its antiseptic qualities were still intact.

With deliberate haste he soaked his bloody bandages, finally peeling them off, revealing the full extent of his wounds. One bullet had sliced across his left side just over the belt line. It had produced a nasty festering wound. The shoulder was another matter. The bullet had entered the back and went out the front. Both holes had been plugged with cloth, but were ugly, red, and swollen.

Using a solution of turpentine and hot water he bathed the wounds and replaced the bandages. The burn streaks on the top of the shoulder and the side of the neck were not threatening, but were tended with care. If nothing else, it reminded Shannon how close he had come to being killed, first in the saloon and later in the store.

Overcome with sheer exhaustion Shannon banked the fire. Then he fell on the bunk, sleeping the sleep of the war weary. Wave after wave of flashbacks, like demons from hell, fragmented his fevered sleep. Dreams of a burning cabin, the raucous laughter of the night riders, the death of his mother and father, a spiraling fall from a cliff, gun muzzles blossoming with flame, and Rachel's pitiable cries for help turned his sleep into a nightmare of surreal remembrance.

Shannon awoke with a start. The cabin was frigid. A few coals from the spent fire sent up tiny wisps of smoke. A howling wind was searching every crack about windows and door. Through the crack at the threshold gusts had blown a long streak of powdery snow across the floor. Easing to the hearth with every part of his body protesting due to soreness and pain, Shannon coaxed the fire back to life.

Water was put on to heat. Rags were stuffed around the door to cut off the chilling draft. Crawling back to the hearth he drank the last drop of warm coffee from the pot. Dried beans had sat cooking in a cast-iron Dutch oven banked with coals for the entire night. Satisfying his hunger with the beans, Shannon again bathed and treated his wounds. They had lost some of their inflamed look and were much better. At last, he slipped underneath the musty covers and slept as one drugged until the next afternoon.

Three days later Shannon was sitting at the rickety table, finishing off the last of the coffee and beans along with a pile of fried side meat. With wounds healing well, he planned and replanned his moves.

Shannon's anger mounted as he thought of the contest ahead. The ranch was not only legally his, but the hopes and dreams of his friends were caught up in that ranch. It was now all-out war; kill or be killed. The most brutal and cunning of tactics would be used. There would be engagements of hit-and-run, ambush, and deception; of dividing the enemy, cutting them off from one another in order to destroy them one by one. How well had he learned this lesson from the Cherokee and the Cheyenne. God help the person who gave aid and comfort to the enemy. That shadowy figure Hall, looming in the background, had to be crushed. There was no other way.

Recourse to the law was not possible. The nearest territorial court was not as he had first thought a hundred miles distant. It was some two hundred miles away. Compounding the problem was the fact that Stillwater had never elected a marshal and was outside the jurisdiction of a sheriff.

Colonel Hall controlled the town and its surrounding territory, by intimidation and force. That which had happened to Hanks and Dobbs, the small ranchers testified to his arbitrary power. It was obvious to any observer that he, in his own twisted way of thinking, considered himself destined to rule over a small empire.

The most dangerous of men in history were not those of smallness in places of great power, nor men of largeness in places of little power. The most viperous of men were small men lording it over little empires. Their sense of self-importance knew no bounds. Everyone and everything about them was imperiled. At times even life was dependent upon their treacherous whims. Such men were challenged only by those of high principle, integrity, and courage, who were ready to sacrifice life and property to right the wrong. Shannon was such a man.

There would be no more avoiding the issue. No more delay or temporizing. No more avoiding engagement in order to fight another day. The time had come to strike. To strike with deadly force and intent.

Shannon finally made his way out of the valley haven, and joined his crew at Rockface. His forces numbered thirteen now that the Haskett cousins had cast their lot with the Bar J. It was a baker's dozen of the best of the best.

CHAPTER 9

Final Battle

Coop finished his inventory of the food stores while Grat checked out equipment and ammunition. The remainder of the crew sat about the campfire, cleaning their weapons. There was little talk. Each waited, in anticipation, Shannon's orders.

For over an hour, a somewhat pale but fully recovered Shannon had been deep in conversation with Ruble, Funk, and the Hasketts. The seven were gathered about the tailgate of a wagon. From time to time pointed fingers moved across the boards creating an imaginary map. Grat and Coop understood what was going on. It was revealed that Funk and Ruble had been high-ranking officers by the end of the late war. Funk had served in J. E. B. Stuart's command, and Ruble had been an officer on Grant's general staff. All three of the Hasketts had been army scouts under the Western Command out of Fort Leavenworth. Clearly they were planning the tactics of the impending struggle with the Slash L. The lantern had burned low and faint streaks of dawn were showing when the seven finally nodded in agreement and returned to the fire.

Shannon, with coffee cup in hand, began to speak slowly. "This is the way it's going to be. First, the Hasketts will scout the Slash L, gaining information on their strength, ranch layout, location of herds, wood lots, and haying meadows. As soon as we hear from them we move."

Grat interrupted, "The Slash L outnumbers our guns about two to one. Don't we need a bigger force?"

Rojas added, "If you get more men, then I need to round up a few more head of riding stock."

"That's one of the really bad things about a range war, more mounts are killed than men," Shannon replied. "These slay-for-pay gunhands will shoot a horse just to put a rider on foot in order to make him an easier prey."

Shannon continued, "I have no desire to bring in hired guns. We have enough men to mount the type of campaign planned. We'll use our brains and guns to match their guns and numbers. Each of you is worth five of them. Check your saddlebags. Make certain you have a pair of moccasins. Little Coop has several pairs already made up. Get a pair from him if needs be. Carry extra ammunition and don't forget your full canteens. If at all possible, leave nothing to chance."

Illinois, with a puzzled look on his face questioned, "Why the moccasins, Shannon?"

"Illinois, we are going to strike in an unexpected way," Shannon replied. "It calls for stealth and the cover of darkness. Not one sound is to be made; once on foot, no boots, no spurs. Get rid of anything that jingles, rattles, creaks, squeaks, or rustles. And speaking of that, I want each of you to oil your harness, every inch of it. If your saddle creaks, place an oiled rag between the saddletree and the leather, if you can get at it. When you see the Hasketts return, be ready to hit the saddle."

Jubal, Jared, and Justus moved like ghostly shadows across the mountains and valleys of the Hall ranch. They split up, each taking a section to scout. On the third day they gathered on the heights above the ranch house to determine the layout and the number of defenders.

One misfortune had occurred along the way. Jared was searching out an unfamiliar canyon that ended in a jumbled rockslide. As he was picking his way out of the twists and turns of the steep-walled canyon his ears caught the slightest sound coming from the mouth of the canyon.

Jared bent low in the saddle, whispered, "Wo, boy," in his horse's ear. The horse stood rock still as Jared strained, with every sense alert, to hear any additional sound.

Minutes ticked by, neither horse nor rider moved. Jared's sixth sense told him danger was just around the bend.

Easing one foot, then the next across the saddle horn, he slipped his boots off, tied them together with piggin' strips, and fastened them to the lariat loop. After slipping on his moccasins he stepped from the saddle to a pocket of jumbled rocks. It was a perfect position from which he could watch the rider who was ever so slowly following his tracks.

Jared picked up a pebble and hit his horse's flank. At the far end of the canyon was a spring and a patch of green. He knew his horse would head for it and wait for his return.

Almost half an hour of patient waiting brought the desired results. A rider came in view. Jared's caution and patience had paid off. His identification of the rider was instantaneous. It was Lon Cafferty, a notorious backshooter, known throughout Texas and the four corners as a sure-thing killer; his rifle was always ready for hire. He always killed from concealment, never facing his victim. He rode slowly, easy in the saddle, with reigns loose. A .50-70 Sharps was resting across the top of his saddle.

Jared waited until Lon was only a foot or two past him. If Lon tried to shoot he would have to twist a quarter turn in the saddle.

Rising to his feet from behind the rocks, Jared spoke, "Lon, drop the gun." Cafferty's response was incredibly swift as he tried to bring his gun to bear on whomever had spoken.

Jared wasn't the swiftest draw but he shot with a deadly accuracy. The Sharps was almost lined up with Jared, when his Colt flashed a wink of impending doom. Lon slumped over his horse's neck and then slid unmoving to the ground.

It was not unusual for lone riders like Lon to be out on the range a week or so. If it was much longer, then a search would be made for the missing man. Since Lon was not a regular hand the Slash L would take its time for a search. This gave the Bar J perhaps a couple of weeks before Hall's men discovered what had happened to him.

Every scouting report indicated Hall felt Shannon to be no great threat. Lessons of history make crystal clear that often the Achilles heel of men such as Hall is an overestimation of their power and an underestimating of the strength of their opponent. Although Shannon and his crew had eliminated some of the Slash L's gunmen, such as Lon Cafferty, Hall felt that at his pleasure he could and would destroy Shannon and the Bar J.

Like murderers who could not conceive of the fact that they would be identified and brought to trial, Hall could not envision the possibility of being defeated. He felt divinely destined to be the victor.

Scouting reports confirmed Hall's apparent contempt for Shannon's strength. His forces were scattered and certainly not vigilant. A work crew of four were cutting wood near a creek almost four miles from the main ranch. They had posted no lookouts, and their rifles were leaning on a log some two hundred feet away. Three groups of two men, each haying in the high meadows and separated from each other by miles, were sitting ducks. Lazing around the bunkhouse were ten gunmen killing time either playing cards or reading penny dreadfuls.

Not one watchman had been posted about the ranch. They were known men. Among them were those who had committed every offense from murder to petty theft. Somehow Hall had scraped the bottom of the bucket, hiring the dregs of humanity. A final head count by the Hasketts indicated the Slash L had twenty riders to the Bar J's thirteen.

The Hasketts drew a crude but accurate map, using prominent landmarks along each obscure trail. The routes were carefully chosen to give as much cover as possible to the attackers. The element of surprise was all-important.

Shannon had instructed the Hasketts to find routes a blind man could follow. This he said to them several times before they left camp. His insistence caused them to wonder just what kind of attack he had planned.

Shannon gathered his men about him and began to explain his strategy. Its primary thrust was to forcefully demonstrate that no Slash L rider was safe night or day. All life and property that could be spared, however, would be. They were to kill only when attacked or challenged by Hall's men. Shannon wanted to strip them of their false confidence, show them there was no refuge, and create within them a fearful helplessness without undue loss of life on either side.

Shannon's group, as well as Shannon, had seen enough of merciless killing and wanton destruction. Most of the men had served during the bloodiest war ever fought. Ruble had lived through the carnage of Anteitam Creek, Funk the horrors of Second Bull Run, Grat the slaughter at Chichamauga, Big Coop the butchery of Missionary Ridge, and Haskett the mangling gory cannon fire of First Bull Run. They all had drunk deeply of the bitter waters of pain, suffering, and loss. They had walked or rode as many leagues through the valleys of death as any of history. They had been touched by the evil of warfare, tried and tested as few men. They knew only one way—fight to win, but to do so as honorably as possible. Shannon had given them a personal reason to fight. The Bar J was theirs as well as his. He wanted them, however, to enter the fray with motives only principled men held sacred.

Of late, Shannon had been churning over in his mind a conversation with Stellwagen during a wonderfully lazy day on the Mississippi. One of the few days when drifting was easy and the mighty Mississippi completely placid.

Stellwagen related the account of a peasant uprising against the oppressive petty ruler of a small fiefdom. This minor prince, as many others like him, controlled a section of the Rhine Valley from a castle overlooking the river.

Each vessel passing on the Rhine had to pay a toll. His greater wealth, however, was wrung from the labor of the peasants who worked his fields and vineyards. They were more slaves than serfs. Their ceaseless labors filled his coffers with coin of the realm.

The day came, however, when they could bear the oppression no longer. By night they struck with scythe, axe, mattock, and adz, killing the tyrant and every member of his household. Not content with their initial victory, they, like sheep killing dogs, broadened their rampage. Every mercenary of the kinglet and their families were slaughtered. The revenge was savage and final. Those innocent along with the guilty were put to death.

An unexpected twist of fate occurred—one not anticipated by the insurrectionist. Rather than being looked upon as champions of freedom, they were viewed with fear and disdain by the vassals on other estates. They had gone too far seeking revenge. What had started based on a lofty principle had ended a matter of uncontrolled personal reprisal. An appetite for freedom had turned into a voracious hunger for revenge. They had become less humane than their overlord.

Shannon wanted his comrades' understanding that killing for revenge alone settled nothing. Should their fight against Hall get out of control, then they would lower themselves to his level, perhaps becoming more evil and destructive than he.

There were not enough pounds of flesh in the world to bring Rachel back. Hall had to be stopped because he held the rights of all others in contempt. He was the stuff of which despots were made. The death of Rachel was nothing more than a visible act revealing Hall's inner evil. Left unchecked, he would continue to destroy anything and everyone who refused to bow down to his authority and the taking of anything he desired possessing.

The owner of the Slash L was but a mere shadow of those of the past who had stamped the pages of history with infamy and human misery—men such as Genghis Khan, Tamerlane, Suleiman the Magnificent, and Napoleon Bonaparte. They all were consumed with dreams of conquest and the establishment of far-flung empires. Certainly Hall was one of the lesser gods of conquest, yet he too had to be thwarted and defeated; if not, the tentacles of his ambitious control would know no bounds. So long as he survived men who tried to live about him with a dream of freedom would be sacrificed upon the altar of his unbridled ego. Those who live with the dream of liberty will not live under tyranny.

It was not just to avenge Rachel's death, the destruction of the ranch, and the killing of Bar J hands that was foremost in the mind of Shannon. Rather it was defending the right to life of Rachel and the Jenkins kid. Both had been the victims of unwarranted violence. There were also his rights and the rights of his men to peacefully and lawfully build a future for themselves.

Beneath scudding clouds, which obscured a waning moon, Grat, Ruble, Funk, and Shannon silently moved in on the woodcutter's camp. A low-burning campfire gave off only a flicker or two of flame. Two men were rolled up in their blankets on either side of the fire. On cat feet Shannon and his men eased into position by the snoring men. In unison, Colts were eased from holsters and nudged against the heads of the sleepers. Each awoke, staring into the muzzle of a .45 or a .44.

"We don't intend to kill you unless you try to do something stupid," cautioned Grat. "Slip out of those blankets. We can do this the easy way or the hard way. We'll slice it any way you want."

One of the men recognized Shannon and Grat from the gun battle in the saloon. He had not forgotten how incredibly fast and merciless they had been in those few seconds. Looking at the others he softly said, "These two cleaned out the saloon in Stillwater. Do as they say or we're all dead men."

Shannon responded, "We are giving Hall an ultimatum. He is to leave this country. He can sell out or be wiped out. My word to you is this. Gather your truck and ride for the far country. You're in over your heads. You don't seem to be the hard cases like that bunch back at the Slash L. If you stay, you could die. If you go, you are reasonably sure of tomorrow's sunrise."

Ruble and Funk shucked the rounds out of the guns and belt loops of the woodcutters, then checked each saddlebag for additional hardware. As they mounted, Shannon put a twenty-dollar gold piece in the hand of each man with the admonition, "Don't even consider going back to the Slash L to get your back pay. This will see you through for a while. Now ride!"

Just before leaving the camp, Shannon carefully placed one twenty-dollar gold piece in plain view where it would be spotted by the Slash L Riders when they came to check on the missing men. Shannon was reasonably certain that the finding of such a coin would be reported to Hall.

The same action was carried out during the night at each of the hay camps by Bar J riders except the leaving of a gold piece. As instructed by Shannon his men left each camp intact. Nothing was removed. After daylight bundles of brush were dragged over the area covering the tracks of those entering and leaving the camps. There remained only one clearly seen set of tracks, those of the Slash L crews leaving the camps.

The Hasketts had reported there did not seem to be one single tracker among the Slash L riders. If this was the case, then Hall would probably jump to the conclusion that his men were deserting him for pay. Else why only tracks leaving and a gold piece left behind.

The Hasketts decided to get in on the fun and games in their own way. Back in the hills they had all attended preaching when handling of snakes was commonplace. They didn't have any personal truck with such but growing up had made some cash providing the snakes.

Jubal had found a rattlesnake den shortly after arriving at the ranch. It was on a sun-baked side of a hill among a jumble of rocks. Rattlers, some six feet long, were sunning on the warm rocks.

Slipping from the ranch Jubal, Jared, and Justus went to the rattlesnake den. Heavy leather chaps covered their legs and boots. Within the hour they had ten of the biggest rattlers in a sack and returned to the ranch.

As Elder Hawkes, the preacher, had instructed them, they milked the snakes of their venom by pressing their fangs over the rim of a fruit jar. Then a nail puller was used to pull out the fangs. Cheats were not only found at card tables in the saloon!

The bunkhouse at the Slash L had a solid plank double door. It had been made that wide to provide space to carry in logs for the huge fireplace which heated the entire building. Each of the three windows had heavy shutters inside and out.

About 3:00 AM, the Hasketts ghosted across the ranch yard. Each carried a stout pole. They eased the shutters closed, and used a pole to securely wedge them in place. Jared slipped to the door and emptied the sack of snakes inside. There's never been a rattler angrier than one whose fangs have been pulled. They hit the floor with a fearsome buzzing. Jubal yelled, "Rattle snakes . . . rattle snakes," slammed the door, flipping a horseshoe through the handles.

It was utter chaos inside. The mad rush to escape was stopped by the blocked door and windows. Yells, cusses, then shots were heard. It would take them hours to locate the snakes, and then they would not be certain they had them all.

By the next day, when no word came from the work crews, Hall sent out riders. They returned with a mysterious account. The crews had vanished. There were no signs of struggle. Wagons, workhorses, along with all harnesses were in place. Tools had been stacked as customary, at the end of the workday. Camp supplies were still in the wagons and blankets spread around a dead fire. A drained coffeepot sat on a flat rock in the fire ring. Only the men and their mounts were missing.

Hall was visibly shaken. In his hand he turned the twenty-dollar gold piece over and over. With each turn of the coin his paranoia increased. Who was buying off his men? If an ordinary hand would walk away after losing a twenty-dollar gold piece, he must have many more! Had all the hands been paid off? Who paid them? Whom could he trust? Shannon was wounded, wasn't he? Someone was trying to destroy him, take away his dreams as always. By leaps and bounds his excessive and irrational suspiciousness and distrust heightened.

Unknown to his closest associates like Norton, the former foreman, and those who had been with him through the war, Hall walked a tightrope between sanity and lunacy.

As Hall paced the floor, a black mood swept over him.

The floodgates of his inner mind burst open, spewing out suppressed memories of the past. A persistent unease held him in a grip. The swirling vortex of the past dragged him deeper and deeper into a fiendish abyss of haunting experiences. In momentary flashbacks he relived each affront, every insult to his inordinate pride or his ego. His shipboard disgrace, Aenid slipping from his clutches, reprimands by the Admiralty court, ostracism by the family, and loss of inheritance, were all due to those who were lesser men like Shaun Murphy.

There were the hours of uncertainty in New Orleans when Washington had learned of his looting of wealth from the residents of the city. Had it not been for a well-paid informer, who sent word of his imminent arrest, he would be in prison. As it was, he escaped westward with a few of his henchmen. There remained barely half of the fortune in cash he had amassed. The memories were haunting ghosts that ran amok in the back alleys of his mind.

Over the years he had been thwarted, foiled by stupid, ignorant people who stood in his way. He held them all in contempt. There was the situation, which arose at Eaton, when the headmaster accused him of unseemly conduct and had him dismissed from school.

He and Lawrence, one of his schoolmates, while on an outing spied a watch in a shop window. Each decided, unknown to the other, to return when the funds were available and buy the watch. Lawrence happened to receive a gift of money from an aunt within the week, and he promptly bought the watch. Every time Hall saw him with the watch his envy and anger grew. Finally during an insignificant argument between the two, Hall turned violent. He picked up a loose cobblestone and smashed Lawrence in the head. Lawrence lived but Hall was shipped home from school in disgrace.

Before that, it had been old Haddington, a family retainer, who could barely sweep the stables due to the infirmity of years and approaching blindness. Hall had been playing with one of the family dogs, a Springer

Spaniel of gentle nature. The play became rougher and rougher with Hall sadistically twisting the ears of the dog. Suddenly the dog snapped at Hall, and he flew into a rage. Picking up a stave, he beat the animal lifeless. When he raised his head from the grisly task, who should be standing there but Haddington with a look of utter astonishment and contempt on his face. Haddington's report to the lord of the manor brought swift and quite severe punishment. Hall fuming with sullen anger swore revenge on the old man. Within the year Haddington died in a fall from a stable ladder. All around wondered why the broken rung appeared to be older and worn thin while the remaining rungs were sound.

The darkest episode of all had to do with the circumstances of his brother's death. Whenever Hall looked at his elder brother, there was a malevolent gleam in his eye. There had been bad blood between the two since childhood. He resented his elder brother's kindly words of advice considering them interference in his life. Hall was constantly in trouble with his brother, a model son, who was greatly loved by his father. It was no case of sibling rivalry; Hall simply hated his brother. That all ended the day the heir apparent died. He was jumping a stone wall when his saddle girth parted, throwing rider, saddle, horse, and field stones into a jumble. It was the younger Hall who picked up the saddle with a partially cut girth, and later burned the girth in a wooded thicket miles from the manor house.

As Hall slipped deeper and deeper into the quagmire of his demented mind, a venomous loathing for Shannon intensified. The full scope of his life's frustrations was focused on him. Shannon's protagonist was slipping the bonds of sanity. He had crossed his Rubicon. He was escaping the boundaries of rationality.

There ensued a lull in the hostilities between the Slash L and the Bar J following the attacks on the scattered work camps. Shannon was content to play the waiting game for a while, but his men were becoming fidgety. They were not the kind to while away the hours.

Grat and Big Coop approached Shannon and said "Shannon, don't you feel that we should get back to the ranch and start making repairs? There's no sense in us cooling our heels here, when we need to be at the ranch. The Hasketts are out there scouting. They will give up plenty of warning in case of an attack." Grat's appeal made sense to Shannon.

A few weeks later the ranch was once again in inhabitable condition. The main house and the bunkhouse had been repaired, stable framing in place, forge roof and corrals restored. Rojas had rounded up some of the stray stock, and Illinois had recovered as much as possible of the garden and grain crops.

For the first time in weeks the men were all well-fed and peacefully sleeping on decent bunks under a roof.

An interlude in the hostilities, however, was all too brief. About midnight the Hasketts came fogging it into the ranch. Jubal delivered the tense message, saying, "Hit the floor and grab your guns. Hall has imported a new bunch of gunslingers, and they are headed this way . . . about an hour and a half away. Should hit just before daylight."

Shannon's men went about their preparations with no loss of motion. Plans had been made for just such a night attack. The men tumbled from their bunks, slapped on their hats, slipped into Levi's, stamped on their boots, and slung waiting gun belts around their waists. Each lifted from the wall rack a Winchester and grabbed a box of ammo from the shelf. Bursting from the bunkhouse they headed for the corrals and remaining hay sheds.

Funk and Ruble were issuing orders, and each man went to his assigned task. From the wagons, hay was scattered in a quarter moon crescent in front of the ranch buildings. Within minutes a mound of hay, some two feet high, stretched at least three hundred yards in front of the ranch house, bunk house, and barn. When the Slash L riders rode in, it would be like riding into the open mouth of a large-sprung U of hay.

Coal oil was sprinkled on the hay, and the men, other than Shannon and Grat, moved to their assigned positions in rifle pits. These had been dug about a hundred fifty yards in front of the buildings along the ranch entrance. Farthermost out were the Hasketts with their Sharps. Shannon and Grat were lying in shallow pits at either end of the hay row ready to light a powder trail from either end of the hay. They settled in to wait.

In inky blackness, the darkest of dark in the hour just before daybreak, the sounds of muffled hoofs could be heard by those in the rifle pits. As Hall's men rode past the ambush, an occasional muted sound was heard. In the dead calm of the night the creak of a saddle or a whisper between riders traveled well. Sacks had been wrapped around the horse's hoofs and tied tightly to avoid any warning to the Bar J. Shrouded in silence they rode into the jaws of death.

When the raiders were within fifty to sixty yards of the straw line, Shannon and Grat fired the powder trail. As it streaked along the edge of the hay, a half circle of fire erupted in front of the attackers. Silhouetted by fire, they didn't have a chance.

The firefight lasted less than two minutes with the sharp reports of Winchesters punctuated by the thunder of the Sharps. Slash L riders were swept from their saddles as round after round spewed from the guns of the Bar J. Three fourths of the raiding party were downed, either killed or wounded. The remainder had no fight left in them. They dropped their guns, dismounted, and stood silently bunched together.

Big Coop broke the silence that came just as a gunbattle ended. Out of the darkness his deep resonant voice boomed like the bellow of a rogue longhorn steer cornered in the brush. "Come, you, sinners, poor and needy. Stand before the Angel of Death and hear your judgment. I'll dangle your wretched bodies over the fires of hell by spider webs, and laugh when they are severed and you fall into the pit of fire." Then Coop let out a god-awful demonic laugh. It was scary enough to raise goose bumps and curl your hair.

The swaggering Slash L "gunhandies" still standing turned into putty. One, who was hardly weaned, kept saying mournfully over and over, "We're gonna die! We're gonna die. We're gonna die."

Shannon, barely able to contain himself, stifled his laughter, and in a voice edged with flint, ordered the survivors to dig graves for the dead. Lanterns were lighted and by daylight words had been said over them. They were buried along the approach to the ranch; their four-by-six mounds of earth and simple plank crosses a warning to others who might think of riding against the Bar J. When the job was completed, the six survivors were taken under guard to Stillwater.

The next day they were put on the stagecoach with the warning if they ever returned, they would join their friends buried back at the ranch. Unless Hall imported more gunmen, he was done for in Stillwater.

Cessation of hostilities between the two ranches extended for weeks after the ill-fated raid on the Bar J. Word reached Shannon that a small group of hardcore hired guns still remained at the Slash L, but their numbers had continued to dwindle. Three had ridden out in the past few days according to the Hasketts. They had dogged them for miles, dusting their heels with well-placed long-distance shots from their Sharps. When the bullets hit too close, they lit a shuck and headed south.

Hall had withdrawn to nurse his wounds and decided what course of action to take. The harsh reality of the situation was finally dawning on him. The Bar J was no pilgrim lash up. It was a formidable opponent not to be taken lightly. Hall was now convinced that Shannon was not only alive and well, but had at his command loyal people of uncommon fighting experience. Every move he made against the Bar J had turned into a disaster. Brooding on this only increased his mental imbalance; besides, his cash reserves had almost dried up.

A fully rebuilt Bar J was more imposing than ever. Rooms had been added to the main house. A wide veranda, whose roof was supported by stone columns across front and sides graced the building, offering a view of the valley that was uniquely pleasing to the eye. The porch was a tribute to Rachel's wishes for the house. She had spoken of sitting out in the cool of the evenings, watching the children play. Whenever Shannon thought of this, his grief became almost unbearable.

Mandy, Coop's wife, had arrived; and the entire crew along with Big and Little Coop joined in a cabin raising. With her motherly ways, she soon won the hearts of everyone on the ranch. She won their stomachs the first week! The third day after arriving she cooked a number three washtubs full of bear paws. Word spread out among the hands. In fact, riders went out to tell those on the range. Within a couple of hours, to the last man, they were lined up at the kitchen door with washed hands, slicked-down hair, hat in hand, licking their lips in anticipation.

Half humming, half singing in a sweet clear voice with a broad smile on her face, Mandy doled out the treats. As the pile of bear paws diminished and coffeepots emptied, Mandy was elevated to the status of divinity.

Mandy brought with her much more than mere cooking skills. She was filled with song and laughter, but most of all loving ways. Mothering, doctoring, listening, advising, cajoling, even threatening in good humor; she brought to the ranch that warm femininity, which touched the flintiest hearts among the men.

It was plain to see that Mandy was becoming the confidant of the men. To her they talked freely of themselves and their past. Mandy never pried into their previous lives, just let them talk. In the West the quickest way to loose friends and alienate people was to probe into their personal lives. People were taken as they were, where they were. Yet from time to time, some of the ranch crew revealed much of their past lives to Mandy. She held these revelations as sacred and cherished them because they indicated her acceptance and trustworthiness.

At times she was shocked as on the day Ruble bared his soul in the privacy of the kitchen while drinking coffee and eating bear paws. He had been the son of a plantation owner in Virginia. Harsh treatment of slaves by an overseer, whom his father would not dismiss even after he had pleaded with him to do so, caused Ruble to leave Virginia and join the Union Army. This was an ultimate disgrace to his aristocratic first family of Virginia and prohibited him from returning home after the war. When Ruble finished his story he sat quietly for a while, his face a mask of misery. "You must have loved your family greatly," Mandy said. Ruble abruptly stood up and went out the door. Mandy watched as he walked grim faced toward the hitching rail, with shoulders braced and a crispness of step. He was blocking out the memory.

On another occasion a tear came to her eye as Funk related his growing-up days. His daddy, a railroad worker, had been a mean drunk who brutally abused him and his mother. During a disastrous episode, Funk's mother was beaten so severely she died. Bloody, whimpering like a beaten animal, his dying mother was curled up in a corner of the two-room shack when Funk walked through the door. His father stood over his mother, bloody belt with heavy brass buckle in his hands, uttering murderous threats. There was no hesitation on Funk's part. As a twelve-year-old gofer on a rail gang he worked as hard and as full a shift of sixteen hours as any man. He was what was called "quick growed." Among the rail crews, young 'uns grew up hard and fast. They sank or swam according to their ability to claw, gouge, and kick their way among men given to cold-bloodied ways.

Funk picked up a butcher knife from the table and sunk it to the hilt in his father's back. He stooped and kissed his dead mother's forehead, stepped over the body of his father, walked out the door and headed to the enlistment office.

It seemed to Mandy that every person had a story to tell, like Illinois when he came into the kitchen to talk with her about the vegetable garden.

"Mandy, have you ever noticed that every plant in the garden seems to have an enemy that tries to destroy it?" Illinois asked. There was no immediate reply from Mandy because everybody knew what he said to be a fact. She thought to herself, *Now what is it he really wants to talk about?*

"Illinois, spit it out," Mandy said. "Is you asking about plants and bugs or folks and troubles? Don't play round and round the mulberry bush with Mandy. My hands is in the dough, the oven is hot, and there are pies to bake. Talk up, boy."

Every hand on the ranch stood in awe of Mandy's perceptiveness. She could cut through the brush to the tree every time.

Illinois thought for a moment, then said, "Mandy, how do you stop hating? I've got a belly full of it and it won't go up or down."

"Land's sakes, child," Mandy said. "If it's that bad, the pies can wait a minute."

"Back in Illinois," he continued, "our family had the finest farm in the whole district. My daddy's brother, Uncle Nabal, lived on the adjoining farm. He was a lazy good-for-nothing bachelor given to coon hunting, drinking liquor, and coveting our farm. Pa died of the pox and Ma just gave up. Uncle Nabal moved in and took over. Within the year Ma wasted away to nothing and died. My two sisters, there weren't but three of us, left within weeks of Ma's death because Uncle Nabal was forever trying to tumble them in the hay. As for me, he worked me like an animal. One night he come home drunk, fell on the bed in a stupor and was instantly asleep. I had had it! I took what money there was from his pockets. Then I loaded my shotgun, ramming a heavy load down both barrels. I pulled the hammers back and put the muzzle to Uncle Nabal's chest. It was going to make an awful mess but I didn't care. Mandy, I couldn't do it, I couldn't pull the triggers. I turned and walked out disgusted with my cowardice and despising him for making me feel that way. That was three years ago. I hate myself for my weakness and him for what he did to my family. It sticks in my craw, Mandy, and I can't get it out."

"Precious Jesus!" Mandy exclaimed. She would do all she could to help him. Illinois was still a little boy reaching out for help in dealing with one of the thorniest problems of life. She wanted to throw her arms around him and hugging him tight tell him, given time, he would find healing. Yet she knew such an act would embarrass him although it was really what he wanted.

Mandy thought, *It would take a lot of listening, encouraging and compassion to help Illinois get the monkey of guilt and hatred off his back.* She didn't know the answer but she could listen.

There was a clearly-to-be-seen sadness in Shannon. All knew of his continuing hold upon the grief of Rachel's death. Most avoided the issue, not Mandy. Although utterly devoted to Shannon, she cut him no slack.

One day she stopped him as he was entering the house with an invitation that sounded not unlike a command, even though gently spoken. "Come, sit a spell with Mandy. You needs a good talking to." Shannon was so taken aback he did as ordered. Somehow he once again felt like a little boy, though now in his late twenties, remembering the times when Aenid, his mother, had caught him in some act of mischief.

"I knows all about Rachel," Mandy said. "Certainly you loved that gal, but it's time you walked away from the grave. It don't stand to reason that you would love a woman who would want you tied to her whether dead or alive. Po' Rachel, she must be in agony. She a' trying to let go and find peace in death and you a' holding on not letting her go. Turn that woman loose so both of you can find peace. Don't set by a grave until you shrivels up and dies. Big Coop and me, we have Little Coop. That boy is our future, you ain't got none."

Shannon's anger rose. How dare she say such things to him? Before he could form a reply, his father's dying words came back to him: "Shannon, you are the only gather me and your ma will ever have. Don't disappoint me. You've got to live. If you die, we are cut off from the land of the living."

The words embedded in his memory, yet forgotten for a while, struck his conscience with convincing impact. If he kept Rachel enshrined in his heart, there would be no room for another. He and his father would be cut off from the land of the living.

Buried deep in the primordial recesses of the minds of men everywhere was belief in a physical immortality, provided their names lived on in male descent. Were there to be no strong sons to enjoy the fruits of his labors and continue the name Murphy? Was he fighting for the ranch just for himself or for his progeny? The last thing Rachel would have wanted was for Shannon to be deprived of the future. Mandy understood all this. He had to let go. As he did, true healing began.

Days of change and uneasy peace settled upon Stillwater. After the spring roundup and sale, Hall's crew dwindled to five. Seldom was he seen in town. Word was he spent a great deal of time away from the ranch; where, no one knew.

Among the strong business leaders of Stillwater there was a growing concern for the future of the town. Within a hundred-mile radius, small ranches were springing up due to the growing demand for beef in the East. Soon a railhead would come to Stillwater in order to ship beef to waiting eastern markets. Right-of-ways had been granted with Stillwater as a temporary terminus. The town had to be prepared for the onslaught of railroad workers, gamblers, thieves, prostitutes, and rowdy trail hands. As equally important were the cattle buyers, the townsfolk, and the established businesses that had to be protected. Boomtowns, such as Stillwater, would be chaotic for a time, never settling down until law and order was established.

A deputation was sent to Washington, petitioning for a territorial federal judge and court to be located in Stillwater. The town agreed to build the courthouse and jail, even to pay temporarily the salary of a federal marshal and deputy. A town council composed of Leiberman; Blanchard, the town doctor; Thordackson, the blacksmith; Callahan, owner of the Palace Saloon; and Woolsley, the schoolmaster, would recommend to the Federal authorities those to be appointed as marshal and deputy.

Shannon called Ruble in for a confab. "Ruble, you know some of the Washington power brokers because you served with many of them during the war. I want you to go with the deputation. Use your influence for the good of the future here."

Ruble's contacts with former friends paved the way for a successful conclusion to their journey. Before leaving the bustling nation's capitol, Augustus Gould, a brilliant young attorney from upper New York State had been appointed federal judge. He was related to a wealthy and politically powerful family, thus assuring him a successful career in the East. Yet he, like so many of the era, was lured to the West. It was a happy choice for as the West grew he would also grow and lend his fortune to its success. Gould was to arrive in Stillwater within two months. The town was instructed to begin building the courthouse and to appoint law officers as soon as possible.

Shannon was both pleased and saddened with the swift moving events. Pleased due to the appointment of the judge, but saddened by the fact that the town council had prevailed upon Al Grat to become marshal. Grat accepted the appointment for a period of two years. All concerned knew he was the logical choice for the job due to his experiences as a guard with Wells Fargo and time spent as a Texas Ranger.

A puzzling incident occurred simultaneously with the celebrations in Stillwater over the coming of territorial justice. Unknown to any in Stillwater, the Slash L was sold to a British syndicate. The first time the town knew of the sale came when its new chief of operations arrived. Hall and his closest henchmen simply disappeared.

Departure of the Slash L crew, however, had not been without notice. All during the cessation of fighting, the Hasketts had periodically scouted the Slash L. Jubal and Jared had, by chance, observed the main ranch when the departure took place. Five heavily loaded freight wagons had left the ranch with three outriders. A small remuda trailed behind. Their route took them by the base of the slope where the Hasketts sat their horses behind a screen of brush and saplings. The Hasketts had carefully studied the drivers and riders through their glasses and as soon as all was clear rode to check the Slash L ranch house. The main buildings appeared virtually empty. Only a skeleton crew came and went from the bunkhouse.

Shannon had urged them time and again to get as accurate a description of the men as possible. Justus had growled more than once about this. One day he stopped Shannon and questioned, "Shannon, why do you have such a thing for the identification of Hall's riders?"

"I'll level with you, Justus," Shannon replied. "Deep down in my bones there's a little shiver and in my mind a slight troubling when I glimpse certain one's of them. You know how it troubles you when you see someone and you get that haunting feeling that you knew them from somewhere? That's the way it is with them. I have the feeling they know something I don't and that disturbs me."

The next day, after consuming one of Mandy's filling meals topped off with fruit and hot buttered biscuits, Jared pushed back and told of the Slash L's leave-taking. When he described the drivers and Hall, Shannon kept pressing for even the minutest detail. The feeling about the riders had first come with the dragging. His fleeting glance of some of the Hall crew before he blacked out stirred his memory. Then, as now, the word portraits painted by Jared failed to produce a positive identification of the men. Shannon shut his eyes, trying to force some concrete recollection. The only result was that vexing feeling which came over him whenever he tried to force recall.

With the passage of time a more relaxed way of life descended upon Stillwater. Sandy McPherson, the syndicate overseer of the Circle K, formerly Slash L, and Scottish to the marrow of his bones, had replaced the old Slash L riders with true cowhands. He, like Shannon, believed in the future of mixed Herefords as the hope of the cattle industry. When the rails reached Stillwater, there would be cattle to ship.

As the herds grew on the Circle K and the Bar J the town kept pace with its own growth. In anticipation of the coming of the railroad, an influx of legitimate businessmen and opportunists took place. The latter quickly learned that Marshal Grat and Judge Gould ran an honest and straight-as-a-die town and territory. Some stayed, most left.

Shannon, however, did not permit his crew to become complacent. Hall, he well knew, had an abiding hatred for him. Although no one had seen him, Shannon was convinced he was still in the area. Every day Shannon carried with him a gnawing unease.

Why, he did not know, but it became almost an obsession to ride out from the ranch two or three times a week, sometimes every day, and practice with his Colt. He had been fast and accurate before but now his gun skills were honed to a fine edge. His draw became a blurred movement. The gun seemed to rise from his holster as if it had a will of its own. The movement was so fast one would swear the gun leapt from the leather to meet his hand. It was one thing to be fast, another to be accurate. Shannon became so focused on the mark he was shooting at that all else faded from view. There came the day when he placed two rolling shots in the heart of a playing card at twenty paces. It was no fluke. He repeated it three times. Shannon was ready.

Shannon called to mind a conversation with Beck after the killing of "Bull" Harkness. He warned Beck to never walk away from a rattlesnake until he had cut its head off and buried it deep. Shannon had no fear of Hall's return. It was a certainty that Hall would try again to kill him. The waiting game would have created tremendous problems for a lesser man than Shannon. He knew Hall was as unforgiving as a rogue wild stallion. He would have to be dealt with sooner or later. In fact, he relished the thought of finally facing him in a showdown.

Daily the Bar J riders were out in the bright autumn days driving the cattle to lower meadows for the winter. Grat and Ruble were working one of the north ranges while Funk and Haskett worked the south and the east. The western high range, the greater distance from the ranch, fell to the lot of Dap and Gin. The gather was running smoothly until Rojas burst into the ranch kitchen with the news that Dap's horse had returned riderless with dried blood on the saddle.

Little Coop was sent out to bring all the crews in from the range, while Mandy gathered needed supplies. Big Coop packed the wagon. If Dap and Gin were wounded or dead, the wagon would be needed for transport. A skeleton crew remained at the ranch as Big Coop, Ruble, Funk, Rojas, and Shannon rode out.

A day and a half later they found the twins' bodies. The ground told the story. They had been ambushed from the rocks and brush not more than thirty yards from the trail. Gin's horse had been killed. A single pair of tracks led from the rocks to the place where the twins fell. The assailant had walked up and shot each of them point blank between the eyes at such close range powder burns covered their faces.

A shared anger gripped every man standing by the bodies. Through their minds ran the thought; how could anyone deliberately shoot into the head of one dead or dying, almost obliterating their faces? To the man they wondered what the reaction of Rojas would be.

For the past year the twins had sided with Rojas, breaking wild horses for the remuda. Others were rounded up and broken to sell in a growing market around Stillwater. They were immensely proud of their small independent venture, which brought added revenues to the ranch. Between the three a strong bond had grown. The twins had been teaching Rojas to read and write. He had been teaching them to read the tracks of men and animals.

As they gathered gear from the dead horse and placed the bodies in the wagon, Rojas sat nearby, his head moving slowly up and down as he offered up an Apache death chant. Before their eyes Rojas was shedding the Mexican part of his nature and was becoming all Apache. Not one among them would have given the backshooters any hope for the future. If they could send them a message, it would read, "Cheer up, the worst is yet to come."

Rojas pulled the saddle from his horse and placed it in the wagon. Taking only rifle in hand he mounted bareback and rode off, leading a fresh horse. No questions were asked, none were necessary. Two or three day's head start for the killers was of no consequence. He would find them in due time.

Five days later Rojas rode into the ranch more dead than alive from wounds, fatigue, and lack of food. Mandy took over the nursing chores. Within the week Rojas was able to sit at the common table. Until that moment he had told no one the account of those five days. Then he spoke freely.

He had ridden one of the horses until it began to tire and then switched to the fresh mount thereby gaining on the killers of the twins with each passing hour and exchange of mounts. He found where the group had split up; three going in one direction, two in another. He followed the smaller group. They were not running their horses; they were walking them like those who felt there was no pursuit. The second night he located the camp of two of the killers. Past midnight he slipped in and cut their throats as they slept. Then he stirred up the fire, heated coffee, cooked, and ate. Then he slept until full light. He recognized both of the men as described by the Hasketts as being part of Hall's party that had left the ranch.

The next day Rojas had discovered the tracks of the other three. They led back in the general direction of Stillwater before veering off toward the Bitterroots. As he sat questioning the whys of such a change of direction, he was knocked from the back of his horse by a rifle blast at short range. It was hours before he regained consciousness, only to find that he had been shot a second time at a point blank range. The bullet had burned a deep furrow across the side of his head. Not more than five feet from him was the body of a rattlesnake cut half in two by a bullet.

He staggered to his feet only to keel over with pain and nausea. His second try was successful. Fortunately his horse, trained to stand where the reigns dropped, was nearby. Those he had been following had quickly ridden away.

Backtracking he found what he had previously missed. Some twenty yards down the trail were slight scuffmarks on a boulder, indicating someone had simply stepped from their saddle to the rock. When Rojas saw it he exclaimed out loud, "You're one dumb Apache. Mistakes like that could get you killed!"

Hidden from sight on the other side of the boulder were footprints leading to the nearby ambush position. On the ground was a Spencer .56-50 repeating carbine shell case. Footprints led from behind the boulder to where Rojas lay on the ground. Apparently, just as the killer was pulling the trigger to shoot him in the head, the rattlesnake buzzed. The shooter must have jerked the trigger as he turned to locate the rattler. Rojas's life had probably been spared by the intervention of a snake.

Shannon's premonitions of Hall's presence was verified. His archenemy was again launching attacks on the Bar J. The months of peacefulness had been shattered by the senseless and brutal killing of the twins and the ambush of Rojas. Ruble, Funk, and Haskett called for a council of war. The issue was simple, totally uncomplicated. It was kill or be killed.

"Take the fight to them," urged Funk. "The longer we wait the greater the certainty of additional losses." Ruble agreed but added a sobering thought. "When we ride out, it will split our forces. We must both attack and defend. Hall must have the ranch under watch. When we ride out, they will probably lead us on a chase away from the ranch then double back and attack."

"That leaves us with one alternative," said Haskett. "Our search and destroy party must be small enough to move quietly and departure should be under the cover of night." They were all in agreement on one point; none were safe as long as Hall's renegades, as well as Hall himself lived.

The thorniest problem would be locating the raider's camp. Rojas indicated it should not be more than two or three days ride from the ranch. That could put it anywhere within a radius of sixty miles. It would take days for a huge search party to locate a camp in so vast an area. There were thousands of acres of mountains and valleys, and the camp would probably be in a highly secluded place. Where was the manpower coming from to make such a search? Every approach would be guarded and tracks leading into the hideout carefully covered.

It was Illinois who suggested a solution to the problem. Seldom did he speak in such gatherings. He had become one of those quiet persons reluctant to speak up. This matter he had churned over in his mind. He decided to throw his two bits worth on the table.

"Shannon, why don't you call on the Cheyenne to help us? You have a good name with them. They respect you. Don't ask them to join in our battle, but to give us information. Parties of braves are right now covering that entire area, hunting meat for the winter. They do not kill near their camps. That game is spared in case of dire need later on. Ask them to send us news if they see such a group, a strange camp, or even cut their trail."

Such a practical suggestion carried its own weight. Before noon Shannon was headed for the Cheyenne village with Little Coop as company. They cut out a few steers and eased them along as a gift for the Cheyenne.

As a long lost brother, Shannon was welcomed at the village, but it was Little Coop that created a sensation. Little Coop had grown to the point that the nickname "Little" was laughable. He stood taller than Big Coop or Shannon and had the bearing of an African prince. The Cheyenne, over whom he towered, identified him with the highly respected name, "Buffalo Soldier." Among the plains Indians no soldier was more highly regarded for their prowess and courage than the Buffalo Soldier.

Little Coop had spotted a pinto mare nearby hobbling on three legs. Walking to her, crooning in a soft voice, he began to gently rub her neck and withers. Caressing the horse ever so gently, he walked around her as she quieted and stood still.

All eyes turned on Little Coop as he took from his pocket a farrier's knife. Lifting the left front foreleg, he saw a deeply imbedded thorn driven almost out of sight in the hoof. Still speaking to the horse in murmurs, he cut through to the thorn opening the abscess that had started to swell. After it burst, Little Coop pulled the bloody thorn.

Little Coop turned his head, looking at Shannon, saying, "Hand me that tin of salve from my saddle bags if you will." He packed the abscessed area with R. and R. Mutton Tallow Salve with carbolic and camphor. Then he patted the horse one last time as he turned away.

Appreciation could be seen in the stolid eyes of every brave watching the treatment. None prized their horse more highly than the Cheyenne, and as horsemen they had no peers. Little Coop had made fast friends of the Cheyenne.

Four days after visiting the Cheyenne village a brave rode into the Bar J. They had discovered the hideaway of Hall's group. It was located three days easy ride from the ranch in an abandoned cabin near Sentinel Gap. It was virtually impossible to see the cabin, since it was located at the far end of a steep-sided blind canyon.

Fearing Hall might pull out before they arrived, Big and Little Coop, Haskett, Ruble, Funk, and Shannon rode with abandon. Following landmarks given, finding the cabin was easy. At daybreak of the third day they had the cabin surrounded. A thin curl of smoke rose from the chimney. In the corral, steamy clouds of frosty breath came from the horses' muzzles. The silence of dawn hung over the canyon.

The first man out of the cabin stretched, yawned, and while hitching up one dangling gallus, he headed for the outhouse. He was followed by another, who stumbled to the porch still stamping on one boot. He walked to the well to draw water.

Shannon's command dispelled the quiet of the morning. "I'm Shannon of the Bar J. You are surrounded. You, outside, plant your feet. You, inside, come out empty handed or die inside. The choice is yours."

No time was wasted in letting the former Slash L riders know they meant business. Before leaving the ranch Haskett had cut several sticks of dynamite and fused them. He struck a match, lighted a half stick, and tossed it into a pile of logs, which had been dragged in for firewood. The deafening roar of the blast bounced from wall to wall of the narrow canyon.

"Come out or be blown out," Haskett hollered. One walked slowly from the outhouse to join his buddy who stood by the well. From the cabin door two others moved onto the porch.

Funk shouted a warning, "Watch out! They've got their hats in their hands." As he yelled the warning, all six of the Bar J guns responded. A fifth man rushed from the cabin with rifle in hand but to no avail. Everybody knew the first thing a cowhand does when he puts his feet on the floor in the morning is to clap his hat on. The two men coming from the cabin had their six-guns hidden under their hats.

Hall's men had not reckoned with the battle-sharpened skills of Shannon and his hands. The first two coming from the cabin never got a shot off and the rifleman only one. Bar J's thundering guns silenced them forever.

"Where's Hall?" Shannon demanded of the remaining two who stood silently by the well. There was no reply, but only a cursory glance told each eye that the hideout was in the process of being abandoned. Five horses remained in the corral. Droppings, however, indicated at least ten horses had stayed at the cabin. Searching the cabin they found no supplies. The five who remained behind had packed their saddlebags and were ready to ride out.

After burying the dead, Shannon's troop rode out with their two prisoners. The two were absolutely closed-mouthed and would give no information on Hall or his whereabouts. The saddles of the dead were put in the cabin and their horses turned loose to join any wild herd they might come upon.

On arriving back at the Bar J, Shannon rested a day and then left for Stillwater with the two prisoners. He would turn them over to Al Grat, swear out the necessary warrants, and leave them to the judgment of Judge Gould's court.

Leaving the marshal's office Shannon dropped in to see Leiberman. Although Leiberman was busy with a drummer selling his wares, Shannon interrupted long enough to invite the storekeeper to meet him at the saloon for a drink.

Leiberman responded, "I'll join you in a minute or two. Make sure Sam gets out a bottle of that Tennessee sour mash sipping whiskey."

The moment Shannon stepped through the door of the saloon he knew he had made a mistake that could well prove to be fatal.

Once again Hall anticipated his moves. Word had reached him that Shannon had taken captives at the cabin. As a result he reasoned that Shannon would bring them into Stillwater and turn them over to the law. All he had to do was to get to Stillwater ahead of Shannon and play the waiting game.

Standing before him at the back of the saloon was Hall. He was barely recognizable. There was a stubble of beard on his face. Shrunken, hollow eyes that blazed with madness seemed to create an evil glow. Filthy clothes hung on his scarecrow body. He was but a mere shadow of his former self. His gun hand, however, was steady and his voice strong.

Shannon was boxed on either side by Hall's gunmen. A darting glance at them brought instant and shaking recognition. Long had their young unbearded faces been vivid in his mind. The years had changed them but not so drastically that Shannon could not identify each of them. He was braced by Tob Messer and Sandy Raisor—two of the men who had killed his father and mother and had tried to kill him. Other pictures flashed through his mind for the first time with crystal clarity. The others in the crowd that had killed the twins and tried to kill Rojas had been Dave Renfro and Tim Kelly. That meant the man in front of him was actually Halstead. Hall was an alias!

Halstead recognized the dawning awareness of Shannon's new understanding. "Yes, I'm Halstead. This time the job will be done and done right. These men from the Smokies have worked for me since I recruited them as a Union officer in Tennessee to capture 'home bounders.' They collected many a dollar of bounty. I paid them well to kill your mother and father, as well as you, but they didn't complete their assignment. Now I get the pleasure of doing so myself. You didn't go down in Leiberman's store. You will this time."

In desperation Shannon tried to think of some subterfuge, some clever ruse, some distraction that would give him an edge. There was no way he could brace all three without taking lead and that would likely be a lethal dose. He came to an instant decision. No matter how many bullets he took, he had to kill Halstead. He had heard stories, verified by eyewitnesses, of men who had been shot several times and still stood to down their opponent. He had to live long enough to destroy the evil personified in this one man.

Concentrate on Halstead, forget the other two, he said to himself. With Halstead dead, the wages would disappear, and with it those who made their living by the gun. They would serve only so long as the money was there. When the well dried up and the bank went broke, they would head for other parts. Then perhaps he, if he lived, could work out his future without interference.

At that moment the totally unexpected happened. Was it fate or chance? Shannon had never believed as most mountaineers that every event of life was preordained, or predestined as in the flinty religious beliefs of the Scotch-Irish. But what happened next would cause him to ponder that possibility.

No notice had been given to a man slumped over at a table in the darkest corner of the saloon, either sleeping or passed out. The voices had roused him, and he silently rose to his feet. When he stepped out of the corner into full light and spoke, all action in the room froze.

"Shannon, boy, is that you? I thought you dead killed by the Cheyenne attack on the freight wagons."

Standing before them was a curly wolf, an apparition out of the past. A mountain man who from his looks was half grizzly and half mountain lion. Long gray hair fell to his massive sloping shoulders. Although shaved, his heavy beard was clearly outlined beneath the skin of a bronzed weather-creased face. Piercing green eyes with pinpoints of fire held a steady gaze on the men flanking Shannon. His long-fringed buckskin coat, high-laced moccasins, huge-cased bowie knife tucked beneath a Shoshone-beaded belt, and low-slung Colt on a plain leather belt sent a message: "Mountain man, beware!"

"Remember, Shannon, I owe you one; that time you took Bull Harkness off my back. Make your play, son, and I'll back you."

Hell's bells, thought Shannon. *Those eyes, that gravely voice, it is Beck!*

Shannon looked at Halstead and quietly said, "You just bought property on boot hill." As he spoke Halstead went for his gun. Shannon had never drawn more swiftly, shot faster or more accurately in his life. It was a split-second blur of movement. The crackling fire of guns filled the room. Shannon's first shot had dead centered Halstead's chest. It drove him against the wall. As Halstead's gun rose, Shannon triggered two more rounds sounding as one, both nailing the frenzied man. He had seen Apache braves high on peyote, who would absorb shot after shot before falling; but he had never faced a man in a crazed state who seemed unstoppable. Halstead appeared to be oblivious to pain. Shannon had to get off a killing shot.

Halstead jerked upright. His gun blossomed fire, and Shannon felt the jolt of the bullet. He was fighting for his life against a demented man who would not go down. Before Halstead could fire again, Shannon's Colt bucked in his hand. This time he shot for the sure kill. The slug caught Halstead square in the Adam's apple, smashing vertebrae and severing the cord of life. Halstead's head dropped to his chest. As he wilted and fell prone, his convulsed hand fired a farewell round into the floor.

Wearily Shannon looked around to check on Beck, Messer and Raisor. Tob and Sandy lay crumpled on either side of him, still in death. Beck was holding a hand to his left shoulder which had a spreading blood stain. Shannon's eyes glazed. His knees buckled just as Grat stormed through the saloon door.

Something is terribly wrong, thought Shannon. The room was growing dark. His arms were wooden and his legs trembling. His body would not do as his brain commanded. He never knew that in one final effort to move, he fell across a table, sinking into unconsciousness.

A lesser man would have died, especially one who had taken four bullets. Shannon's strong will to live and rugged constitution coupled with Mandy's nursing, feeding, and badgering had accomplished part of a miracle. Doc Blanchard had done the rest.

All on the ranch had heard Shannon's complaining that Mandy had poured so much chicken and beef broth down his throat that he would soon be cackling like a hen in the morning and bawling like a calf in the evening. Sealed with gratitude in his mind, however, was recall of those first painful days after the gunfight when Mandy sat in a rocker by his bed day and night. Every time he waked Mandy would be standing over him, feeling his fevered brow or placing a cool damp cloth on his forehead.

The fact that Beck had decided to stay the winter caused Shannon to fight even harder to gain his strength. The sooner he was up and about, the quicker would come the time when they might catch up with the events of the past years. Beck was the closest thing he had as a father figure since leaving the Smokies. For certain, if at all possible, he intended to prevail upon Beck to join the Bar J. He could have the share of either of the twins.

Winter came with its transforming ways. Skies of blue were daubed gray. As far as the eye could see nature's paintbrush enameled the world a glistening white. Grating, jarring, penetrating sounds were muffled to pleasantness by creation's mutes. It was a time of bone-chilling cold. Every cowhand rode with upturned coat collar and scarf or bandanna over their hat and tied under the chin to ward off frostbite from the ears. Water holes for the cattle had been cleared of ice and hay scattered from ricks. Before the first storm came, the herds had been brought down from the highest ranges to lower, more protected valleys. The mixed Herefords were real survivors, and needed to be, for the winter was fierce. The snows were not so heavy but the cold was intense. The jaw-quivering, body-shaking wind-driven cold was unreal. It was a harsh time for men and stock.

Silence hung heavily over the ranch. Hearing sounds outside, Shannon moved from his chair by the fire where he sat talking with Beck, and went to the door. Looking out he saw several Cheyenne braves astride their quietly standing horses. Shannon walked across the porch and into the ranch yard to greet them. This was their first visit to the ranch since it had been established.

Much to Shannon's amazement the spokesperson was a woman, soon identified as the adopted daughter of war chief Night Wolf. Her English was flawless. Her mother, as a young girl, had been captured during a wagon train raid. Though born among the Cheyenne she went to a mission school. She had attempted to live among the whites but was blatantly harassed by base men of both high and low estate. Finally she returned to the Cheyenne where her lot was greatly improved by the high regard in which the Cheyenne held their women.

A problem arose when she defended herself too well with a knife. One of the braves sought to force her sexual favors, thinking he would be guiltless since she was a half-breed. Refusal on the part of an unmarried half-breed woman was a tremendous blow to her aggressive admirer's ego.

Had Water Song been a full-blooded Cheyenne the brave would never had made such advances. Among no Indian society were women held in higher esteem than among the Cheyenne. In Cheyenne lore, it is affirmed that as the women of the tribe went so went the tribe. "A nation is not conquered until the hearts of its women are on the ground then it is finished no matter how brave its warriors or how strong their weapons."*

The incident was firmly handled by a solemn council of tribal elders. A brave's death at the hand of a woman, who was not full-blooded Cheyenne yet who lived under the protection of the Chief, was a matter of deep concern. The Cheyenne had the deepest of respect for the wisdom of the elders as well as the sacred customs, which had historically kept the tribes intact.

---

*   Author unknown. Part of the Cheyenne oral tradition.

For hours consideration was given to the fate of Water Song. It finally was reduced to one issue: Would or would not the council ban Water Song, ostracizing her from the tribe, banishing her forever? Night Wolf rose to speak.

"Water Song is destined to help us survive as people. That is why I adopted her as my daughter." His next words brought an awed silence. "There came to me a vision in the night, of which I have not spoken until this moment. A vision of Water Song standing by the side of a white man, pleading the cause of the Cheyenne before the gathered chiefs of the whites. As chief of the Cheyenne I could be nothing less than faithful to my vision." Then I heard a voice saying, "Words are more powerful than weapons." Thus Water Song was spared.

Shannon's insistence that they join him in the warmth of the house fell on deaf ears. Water Song spoke to Shannon, "We must talk of your agreement with the Cheyenne."

He replied in Cheyenne so the braves would understand as he spoke of the accord reached years previously. "I promised your tribe that when there was need for meat in their lodges, it would be here for them." Pointing to cattle in a lower grazing area about a quarter of a mile from the ranch house. Shannon continued, "There are almost a hundred head in that bunch. Cut out what you need for your people." He spoke apologetically to Water Song. "My herd is smaller than expected due to the raids of my enemy, Hall. Know, however, that my word once given shall not be broken. You are welcome to share in what we have."

There were nods of approval. All of the braves slowly turned their horses heading for the cattle.

Shannon actually found himself staring at Water Song. Her light bronze skin seemed to glow in the brilliant light of the winter's day. This caused her ebony eyes to appear strikingly larger and more luminous. Her face, beneath the wolf fur hood, was framed with jet-black hair that shone like the feathers of a raven. When she smiled, her full lips parted, revealing evenly matched snowy white teeth. It was a strong face radiating sheer femininity. That with a voice which was soft and lilting could set a man thinking thoughts perhaps he shouldn't think. It was as if Water Song could read his mind. A mischievous smile raced across her face and her dark flashing eyes seemed to sparkle brighter as she spoke.

"As 'Ghost Who Walks in Moccasins' and as Shannon you are known among the Cheyenne. We know of your struggle with Hall and the losses you have sustained. You are a man who honors his word." For at least a minute she continued stating the laudable merits of his character.

As the words or praise flowed, Shannon began to feel more than a bit chesty. Nothing more quickly swells the male ego as compliments from a beautiful woman. With an impish look she concluded with, "Shannon, aren't you a little bit ashamed to look at a woman that way, undressing her with your eyes?" In her voice was no hint of anger or offense. The words were spoken quietly but there was a happy undertone of sheer deviltry in her voice.

With the concluding word she turned her horse to ride away. Shannon's anger flared, but only for a moment. Then he burst out laughing. She had blind-sided him with womanly wiles as old as creation. She had led him down the glory trail of flattery and then rapped his knuckles like those of a naughty little boy. Shannon thought to himself, *Why, with that woman you could ride the high lonesomes.* In the distance as Shannon's laughter reached her ears, she too began to laugh. It was a beginning.